Why Get Up In The Morning

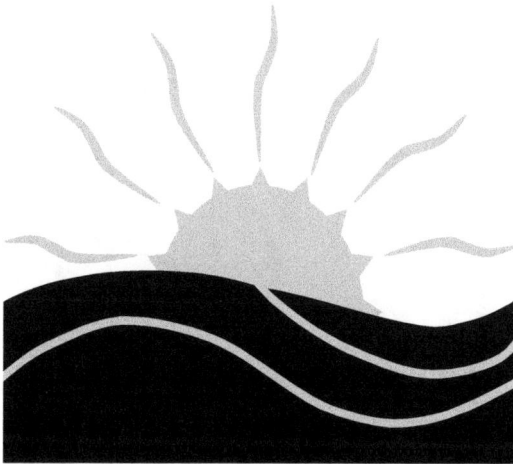

WHY GET UP IN THE MORNING

A Guide to Meaning in Life

by

Tom Kramlinger

WHY GET UP IN THE MORNING

Published by:

The Word Potter
363 W Lake Faith Drive
Maitland, FL 32751

Dedication

To John Williamson

A colleague and mentor, whose
journey was short, but whose lantern
burns bright.

WHAT IS LIFE?

Life is a gift	accept it
Life is adventure	dare it
Life is a mystery	unfold it
Life is a game	play it
Life is struggle	face it
Life is beauty	praise it
Life is a puzzle	solve it
Life is opportunity	take it
Life is sorrowful	experience it
Life is a song	sing it
Life is a goal	achieve it
Life is a mission	fulfill it

Author unknown

Table of Contents

Introduction

Part Three—The Road of Salvation

Part Four—The Realm of Being

Conclusion

Acknowledgements

I gratefully acknowledge the authors and publishers who have granted permission to reprint the texts cited in this book. I thank my manuscript readers, Don Goergen, O.P., Kathleen Whalen Fitzgerald, and Cyril A. Reilly, for their input, and especially David McNally and John Enright for their continued encouragement. Finally, my wife, Maureen, for her insights, inspiration and experiences.

INTRODUCTION

A Night in the Cemetery

When I was 14 years old, Phil and Ronnie dared me to spend a night in Roselawn cemetery. We slipped through the gate at dusk when no one would see us. We traveled light—just flashlights, some snacks and our sleeping bags.

"Where should we set up?" I asked.

"Over here by the fountain," Ronnie suggested.

"No," said Phil, "Let's sleep out by the graves, to prove that we really did it."

So we unrolled our sleeping bags in the deep heart of the cemetery, where the most headstones poked up in the gathering gloom. We joked a lot to bolster our spirits.

"Did you bring the garlic?" someone asked.

"No, why?"

"To scare the vampires off."

"Don't worry. You don't look like you have enough blood left to attract even the thirstiest."

"Shush! Listen! Do you hear anything?"

"No. C'mon, it's just your imagination."

"Oh yeah. Well how about this?" Ronnie opened his mouth and barked the most piercing werewolf imitation I ever heard. "Arf, arf, arf, aarrrrouuuuuuu. Arf, arf, arf, aarrrrouuuuuuu."

"Jeez, whose side are you on?" Phil complained.

As the darkness thickened we grew accustomed to the graveyard. Nothing moved, and the earth didn't swallow us up. We started examining the gravestones with our flashlights.

"This guy must have been one of the pioneers. Look, 1857."

"Here's one that was only three weeks old."

"This lady was a nurse in the first world war."

One engraving caught my eye. "Look at this," I said. "It tells something about the guy—more than when he lived and died. 'In all things he strove for excellence.'" We all stared at it for a minute. Finally, I said, "What do you think they'll say about you, Phil, on your gravestone?"

"He shit his pants in Roselawn cemetery," crowed Ronnie. He tumbled in the grass and gasped with adolescent laughter.

"No, seriously," I said.

"I don't care," said Phil, "as long as it's a hundred years from now."

We got through the night without much damage. The dew soaked our sleeping bags and some chipmunks chewed our granola. We took the event to mean that we were brave and had nothing to fear from life—or death.

I often remember that night. It wasn't just the bravado that counted. There was also the enduring humanity of our hosts. I realized that a cemetery isn't a scary place or even just a resting place. It's a place of human significance where each monument bravely proclaims who this person was.

The Search for Meaning

I still go back to visit cemeteries, especially when I am riding my motorcycle through the countryside. I like to stop at small churchyards and wander from stone to stone to learn about the meaning of people's lives. I think about what I would like written on my own tombstone. One I particularly liked was chiseled on greenish slate in the "Old Burying Ground" just off Lexington Common, where the first skirmish of the American Revolution was fought. It declared of Amos Marrett who died in 1805 at age 66:

Here lies the man who was both kind and free
Whose heart was filled with God-like charity

I liked that. I hoped it summed up old Amos' life; not just the sentiments of a pious stone cutter. The older I get the more I care about things like that: What are the themes that give meaning to life? What do people live and die for? I want to know if we can take hold of meaning, claim it and name it. Or is meaning so mysterious that we can only capture it mutely in the space between the dates on a headstone?

What about you? Do you care about meaning in life beyond meeting your daily needs? Are you interested in why people get up in the morning and what they dedicate their lives to? Or do you want to know more about the meaning of your own life? What will people remember when you are gone? What will they inscribe on your headstone?

Are You Like Dave and Susan and Grace?

A few years ago I attended a peace gathering in the basement of our community center. About ten of us sat in a

3

circle in the dimly lit room. We each held a small abrasive stone to represent the irritations that lead to war. Eventually, the conversation turned to the personal wars that really drew us to the meeting.

Dave was about forty-five, a little gray, and clearly a no-nonsense business man. He explained his participation with surprising candor. "I think I need this," he said, "because I've been a pretty hard taskmaster all my life. All I've cared about is making my business go right. I think it's been hard on my family. That's why my wife dragged me here tonight. Isn't that right, Barb?"

"Dave is a good man," Barb explained, trying to laugh at the same time. "But I have to tell him over and over not to treat us like employees. Children and wives don't come with job descriptions."

"I'm beginning to see that," Dave continued. "But what really bothers me, my 'stone,' is that maybe I've looked at life too narrowly. 'Shallow Dave' is what they call me at home when they really want to get me. That's what I'm afraid of becoming. And that's why I'm here tonight."

"What I'm afraid of," said Susan, an outgoing young woman, "is being aimless. I try to do what everyone tells me is right, like coming here tonight. But I don't know what is really right, or where I'm really going. Last week I had to write a resume for a job, and I didn't know what to say. After I said I went to Fillmore Grade School and Central High School, what else was there? I hadn't won any honors or starred in athletics or anything like that. I want to do something important with my life but I don't know what it is."

Another participant was Grace, a gentle lady in her sixties. She didn't speak until the end. "My brother is dying of cancer," she said. "Every time I see him I want to hug him and talk about what we did when we were young. His dying makes me think about my own life, how I frittered it away. I wish I could bring it together somehow. Right now, I just look at old photo albums and feel sad."

My heart went out to Susan and Dave and Grace. They were wrestling with questions about the meaning of life. I wanted to respond to them, but I felt strangely unable to speak.

It seemed so obvious to me that life has meaning. So what kept me from speaking? After all, I'm the one who hangs around cemeteries thinking about these things. I've also enjoyed years of education, debate and reflection. I've studied the great philosophers—Plato, Aristotle, Descartes, Hegel, Wittgenstein—and I've traveled far to listen to holy men like Vinoba-Bhavi, the Chini-Lama, Aurobindo, and Teilhard de Chardin. So why couldn't I think of something to offer?

I didn't sleep very well that night. It was the stones. Somehow they got under the mattress. And my own stone was the lumpiest of all. Why couldn't I speak with those people? Was it a lack of clarity? Or maybe a lack of courage?

In the morning I made up my mind to write this book. It's for Dave and Susan and Grace. It's also for you because I imagine that in some ways you are like them. And it's for me—to find both the clarity and the courage I lacked that night.

The Purpose of This Book

Here's what we're going to do. We're going to explore the world of meaning. Not the way professional philosophers do, but in a way that works for ordinary people like us. The professional philosophers emphasize logic, analysis, cosmology and systems of thought. And to some degree they are right. But *real philosophy* is something more personal and useful. It is the reason we give ourselves to get out of bed in the morning. It is our natural urge to make sense out of life and find meaning in one of the many splendid avenues that are open to us.

So the purpose of this book is to examine themes about the meaning of life and to offer some ideas about how you and David and Susan and Grace and I can lay claim to our own personal meaning—something to live by, something to write on our headstones.

The Yellow Brick Road

What we'll do is go on a journey. It will take us through three realms, like the *Divine Comedy*. The realms, however, will not be Dante's Hell, Purgatory and Heaven, but what we will call Having, Doing and Being. These names were invented by famous philosophers like Plato and Sartre, but I hope by the end of the journey you will find them as familiar as your own neighborhood.

Actually, our path will be rather like the Yellow Brick Road in the *Wizard of Oz*. It's a colorful road that meanders through life and leads to a wonderful end. Dave will be the Tin Man, a good person, but "shallow," looking for his heart. Susan can be Dorothy, the effervescent, searching youth. I'm not sure who Grace is—maybe Aunt Em who's tired of sitting at home letting life go by. I'll be a combination of the wizard who knows something about the way and the cowardly lion who struggles to lead. And you will be the guest of honor.

The Roadmap of Meaning

Here is the roadmap. We'll start down the wide part of the road where the most people travel. This is the realm of Having. It's colorful and chaotic here. A sense of hubbub is everywhere. That's because meaning in this realm comes primarily from relationships to the changeable things of this world. In the wonderful bazaar of Having we will explore the kaleidoscopic meanings that people find in their relationships—with other people, their possessions and the structures of society.

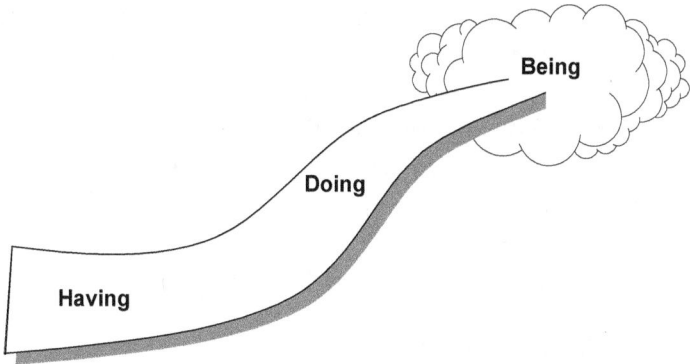

Next, we'll turn sharply up the path that leads through the realm of Doing. The grade is steep and requires effort to ascend. This is where people find meaning primarily in their action. Here we will examine themes like making a contribution, acting nobly, and changing the course of history. There are fewer people in this realm, but still a great number. They tend to be quite busy and determined, so don't get in their way.

Finally, we will take the road which is truly less traveled. It is the path of scholars, mystics, and poets that winds through the realm of Being. We will walk carefully here, exploring forms of meaning whose names are presence, knowledge, becoming, communion, and transcendence.

I will also point out a parallel road called the way of salvation. It too passes through all three realms, and we can detour there at any time. Our itinerary calls for a side trip there just between Doing and Being. What's special about the path of salvation is the sense of being rescued. It's as if the road of life runs along a cliff there and one is constantly aware of being saved from falling off.

Both Secular and Religious

Please notice that the road of meaning is both secular and religious. If you keep your eyes steady, you will see the secular dimension—the meaning of life in natural terms, without reference to God. If, on the other hand, you look again (with belief in God), you can see the *same* meaning in its religious dimension. For example, as a gift from God. You can choose whichever dimension you prefer. I just invite you to notice that *both* are there and both are worthy of respect.

The Multiplicity of Meaning

One of my fundamental beliefs, a point where I differ from many others, is that life has *many meanings*. As you get ready to come along, please be aware that we are *not* going on a search for the *one true* meaning of life.

In my view, life is a riot of meaning! There is not a single meaning for everybody. Nor is there necessarily only one meaning for each of us. We are all prolific philosophers. It's our nature to see and invent meaning. If we turn down some doctrine offered to us, we take up another. We tell ourselves stories; we propose explanations; we fight for values; and we make commitments. And if we don't talk about our meaning in words, we live it out in deeds.

The problem with meaning is not that there is one true meaning that is hard to find. The problem is that there are so many meanings that it is hard to sort them out.

Shopping for the Most Valuable Themes

Yet certain *themes* emerge from this multitude of meaning. Our minds tend to adopt these themes in the same way that the main road tends to follow the river in the valley and the pass between the hills. My purpose is to describe a number of the more common and valuable themes—the *archetypes* of meaning. I want you to see enough examples to appreciate the variety to choose from, yet not so many that you lose track or conclude that the choice doesn't matter.

Most people adopt two or three primary themes of meaning for their lives. They may appreciate and experience many, but they dedicate themselves only to a few. So our journey will be something like a shopping trip in which I point out the most prized treasures. You may examine as many as interest you. But you will probably "purchase" only a few. That's because the purchase will cost you something. To adopt some theme as a principal meaning requires a certain dedication on your part. But let me not prejudice you there either. Take as many as you like.

Some Attributes of Meaning

Some of you may be wanting a definition of "meaning." Others, like Dave, may be falling asleep or anxious to get moving. So I will keep this short. In searching for meaning, we are looking for something that is:

1. **Intense, Personal Experience**—Meaning is something we get when we are most awake. It's personal and intense. It doesn't happen when we are asleep. It's not like a law of physics that operates whether we realize it or not. Meaning happens to us *as persons*. Whether all in a flash or slowly mulling it over, we appreciate meaning—not as a general truth, but as a *truth for me*.

2.   **Larger Than Self**—Living only for oneself is fine, but I don't think it gives a deep sense of meaning. Meaning, in most of the themes we will look at, calls for a commitment to something outside oneself—a person, a cause, a principle, a divinity. Human meaning thrives in long-term realities and whole-hearted commitments.

3.   **Intelligible**—Meaning is something we grasp with our minds. We may not fully understand it, but it has the ring of logic to it. Some pattern falls into place. Some missing piece is found. Some whole is made complete. The logic may not be perfect, but it is essential. Otherwise our minds would not agree that something has meaning. Thus, if there is no justice in life, there must at least be poetic justice. For life to have meaning it has to make sense.

4.   **Purposeful**—Meaning is always just beyond us—not quite fully in our grasp. It's something we hold, yet it draws us on. It gives us hope. If we fully possessed it, it might no longer be human meaning. That's because human consciousness constantly moves forward. Meaning gives us a reason to get up in the morning and spend energy. It provides a sense of purpose. It promises something valuable still to come—something yet to have, to do, or to be.

5.   **Noble**—Some principles that people live by are rather narrow in scope. Examples of these are:

   - "He who dies with the most toys, wins."
   - "Every night a new conquest."
   - "At least I weren't no trash."
   - "I finally got even with them."
   - "I never went to bed hungry."

Real meaning is about noble and uplifting themes, the ones that most people would be proud to announce on their memorial stones. As for these others, I acknowledge their power to motivate, but we will not examine them further on this journey.

Some Assignments

Now for our assignments. Dave loves this part, since he has a job description for everyone.

My job will be to guide us along the road. I will explain the features of each type of meaning and suggest why it might be important to you. To illustrate I will tell some stories. Most of the stories come from my own experience; some are from literature; and others were told by friends. Where appropriate I have changed some names and circumstances.

After walking around each theme of meaning, I will ask you to reflect on your reaction and evaluate to what degree this meaning appeals to you.

You can design your own job description—anything from putting the book down now to thinking about it all the time. But here is what I recommend:

1. Examine each idea with a fresh mind and open heart. If you want to get full value out of this journey, then suspend (at least temporarily) your assumptions about the one true meaning for you until you have taken a good look around.

2. Ask yourself how you have experienced each kind of meaning, or how you might experience it in the future.

3. Take note of what attracts you so that you can review it later by yourself.

4. Give yourself an answer when I ask you a question. The more you think out loud, the better.

5. Argue with me or with different parts of yourself. If you don't agree with something, stop and shout. Slam down the book or write something in the margin. It's your philosophy we're talking about here, so you need to debate about it.

6. Don't criticize what others find meaningful. If something doesn't attract you, fine. Just put it back gently for the next person, the way you would carefully replace a crystal goblet you choose not to buy in a china shop. It will be precious for someone else.

7. Do the exercises. You'll be surprised how much brainpower you have in your fingers when you set them to writing.

8. Skip around if you like. This book has all the structure of a shopping list. Except for this chapter and the conclusion, it doesn't have an argument to follow. You can read it from back to front if you like. I'll be happy to join you anywhere along the way.

9. Compare yourself to Dave, Susan, Grace and others we meet along the way. They represent different aspects of our deeper human nature: male and female, old and young, assertive and quiet. Wisdom comes partly from resonating with the experience of others.

10. Go on by yourself after we conclude. In the end only you can tell your story, or compose your real epitaph.

The Pot of Gold

At the end of the journey we will take stock. I hope there will be a big payoff for you, a spiritual pot of gold. I hope by then that the Dave in you will say, "Wow, I never realized how deeply meaningful my life has been." I hope the Grace in you will cherish every minute of life and want to share it with friends. And I hope the Susan in you will face the future with excitement and a sense of direction. As for me, I hope that the courage to speak will be its own reward.

There is another benefit to look for—understanding our companions. Sometimes we get frustrated with people who are not like us. We can't figure out what make them tick. Perhaps this journey will give you a deeper insight into the motivation and values of the people you live and work with.

THE REALM OF HAVING

We start our journey by stepping into the Realm of Having. It's one of three dimensions that philosophers from Plato on have described as a realm of meaning. It's a lively, colorful place, not unlike Disney World or Busch Gardens. Thousands of people are milling around. We see shops filled with attractive things and stages where people perform. Costumed characters entertain us along flowered paths. Police, sidewalks and traffic signs keep order. There are benches where people rest and watch each other, and restaurants where they sit with friends to eat something and share their treasures.

This is the realm where people find meaning in *what they have* and *who they are with*. It's the realm of give and take, of law and order, of being in relationship with the good things and good people of this world.

He is a great and
righteous person
who loving himself,
loves all others
equally.

Meister Eckhart

HAVING SOMEONE TO LOVE

Let's start with love. When I ask people to describe their life's meaning, the theme most frequently mentioned is love, and especially family love. Dave, Grace and Susan all spoke about it. Grace was losing it, Susan still looking, and Dave afraid that it was all he could think of. "Of course I love my family," he said. "Don't we all? Isn't that just part of being shallow?"

Love may be common, but it is far from shallow. It is perhaps the most profound form of meaning in the realm of Having. That's because it consists in having an intimate relationship with the most wonderful beings in the world, namely, other people. Relationships with things are meaningful, as we shall see, but relationships with people are especially meaningful because both parties are a constant source of novelty and interaction.

When you are in love, you do as much giving as receiving. This exchange is the essence of the relationship. You have each other. And what you get is not just a companion, but the whole world as seen by the other.

For some of us, this experience happens with many persons; for others, with only a few.

17

Mama D's Expansive Love

I think of "Mama D," an Italian lady who runs a restaurant near the university in our town. To me she represents those for whom love is the ultimate meaning in life. I heard her give a talk once on Mother's Day. "You love you' mama, and you' mama love you," was her message. This is what sustains hundreds of thousands of human beings—a faithful love—for spouse and for family.

Mama D also loves spaghetti and serves a pretty good batch of it at her restaurant. Not only her personal family counts for her, but hundreds of clients as well, from well-heeled celebrities whose pictures cover the walls to poor university students whose homework covers the tables. Hers is an expansive love—as if one family alone were not enough to receive it. You feel good when you go there, because her kind of love creates an unspoken welcome. Hers is a "go out and get 'em" kind of love. It is a love that not only gives meaning to her life, but seems to add something to the lives of others as well.

Madame DuFour's Man

On the other hand, there is Madame DuFour. What I remember best is her devotion to her husband, a French baker. I met her in the late 1960's when I was studying in Paris. She was the concierge of my building. I wasn't able to converse nimbly on many subjects in this new foreign language, but it wasn't hard to know what Madame DuFour was saying. The subject was always the same—her wonderful deceased husband and how much she missed him. Of course, she talked about the weather, the misplaced key and the rules of the house. But when it was time to say something important and personal, it was about "her man," how good he was, how he worked from before dawn to the end of the day, and how devoted they were to each other.

Madame DuFour's life was very contracted. She was old and didn't move quickly, especially when I needed her to make a phone call or open the back gate. Not that she was unkind or unwilling, just slow and stiff. So was the range of her love— she opened slowly the gate of her heart to let anyone in or out.

If Mama D's love was outgoing and inclusive, Madame DuFour's love was inward and exclusive. But I think of her love as deeply meaningful. Her love for the baker *was* the meaning of her life. Her love, though narrowly focused, was intense.

I see two funerals in my imagination. Mama D's attended by hundreds of people on a sunny day with many flowers and much oratory. And Madame DuFour's: simple, in the rain, attended by two nieces and a priest. And yet the headstone of each may say the same: "She loved deeply. May she rest in eternal love."

The Family Man

For most people, the family is the right range for loving relationships. There is a special meaning that comes from having a place in the middle of a vibrant, interacting family. At least that's what my uncle thinks.

He is in his middle sixties, works for a bank, and lives in a modest house. "I grew up in a family of five," he said one night over a cold beer. "There were four boys and my sister, Lou. Ma and Dad were simple people. I guess I'm just a simple guy myself. Ma was born on a farm in the 1800s. Then she came to town and met Dad. He worked for the railroad all his life, fitting pipes on steam locomotives. Every day he walked to the yards carrying a big black lunch pail. Sometimes in the evening we kids would wait for him to see if he brought us anything. We'd walk with him from the corner. Then at the front porch he'd open the pail. Usually there were just scraps of metal he'd picked up at the shop. But sometimes there was candy. Dad never said much, but we knew that he loved us.

"One of our family routines occurred every Thursday afternoon. That's when Ma's sisters got together. They took turns meeting at each other's houses. When it was at our house, I'd sometimes hide in the stairwell so I could overhear their conversation. They often talked about Aunt Emma's Andy, about his drinking and all the trouble he got into—like when he got fired for stealing a truckload of playground equipment from the school where he worked. Poor Aunt Emma. She needed those Thursday afternoons more than the others. Their loving attention helped her accept her life.

"Every summer we'd spend a week or two at the farm owned by Ma's cousin, Peter. It was north of town about thirty miles and we took the train up. Dad, of course, always got free passes. It was good to see how we were related to Uncle Peter and his family. In those days there were hostile feelings between city people and country people. They used to sneer at each other and call each other "bumpkins" and "slickers". It was nice to know that we were both a city and a country family. We were the best of both.

"Our close feeling didn't come right away though. I remember once watching Uncle Peter milk the cows. I knew that milk came from the udders and was squeezed into pails. But I couldn't figure out his method. 'What are you doing with the string?' I asked. 'Are you tying the nipples?' I always pictured that the milk came out in big drops and not that it streamed out like, well, white string. Uncle Peter almost fell off his stool laughing. 'That's the milk,' he said. 'What strange ideas they teach you in the city about farming.' He was kind enough not to call me a dumb city kid. He put the blame on what 'they' teach. Later Uncle Peter sat me on the stool and showed me how to 'make string' myself. His kids taught us how to jump down the haystack and chase cats in the barn. Doing stuff like this made us all one big family.

"It's not just me that feels this way. My sister once made a quilt out of pieces of cloth that came from every branch of the family. She sewed them all together and embroidered our names on them to show how we all fit together. And my brother has pinned up hundreds of family photographs on the wall in his basement. Of course he picked some of the worst poses. Cousin Jeanie in a bathing suit when she was pregnant with Mark. And Aunt Emma with watermelon seeds on her chin. We're all there, looking our best at weddings and our worst at picnics. There's an ancient tintype of Great Grandpa, proud and somber on a horse. And the generations go down to my own granddaughter, Erin, bawling her head off on her first birthday.

"When I look at my life, that's what it's all about—family. I don't have much of a job, just arranging mortgages at a bank. It's OK. It helps people. It helps them start their own families, I guess. But what's important is being part of a big family. I liked growing up in one, and I liked watching my own kids grow up. And now they're having their kids. Maybe someday I'll be the patriarch of a great dynasty." At this he laughed.

"What do I want engraved on my headstone? I don't care. My name, I guess. What I really care about is being buried in the family plot, surrounded by all my relatives."

Questions for Reflection

Who are the people you care about? Are they many
or few?

What do you share and exchange with them?

How has your place in what you count as family changed
over time?

Have you found the limits of your love, or is it still expanding?

*Sometimes you
wanna go where
everybody knows
your name*

Cheers Theme

BEING CARED ABOUT

Moving further along our journey, we pass a tavern where two young women are whispering on a bench. From their gestures and glances it's easy to see they are talking about the young men seated across the courtyard. Their situation brings us to another form of meaning. It's like the meaning of love, but the other side of the coin. It's the experience of *being* loved. And even more, it's the experience of being loved by someone whose love really counts.

When I was in junior high school it didn't matter that Florence and Virginia had a fight in the cloak room about who would marry me. Neither did it count later that Jackie had a crush on me. I didn't care about any of their love. I only cared about what Sherry felt. If *she* loved me, then every moment was enchanted.

Too many seekers of meaning the exquisite moment comes from knowing that they have been especially chosen or noticed by someone whose favor really matters.

To Be Loved by God

One summer night I was standing in a big yard near a cornfield. I smelled the corn in the warm, moist air. It was a dark night. There was no moon and no horizon to separate earth and sky. The stars seemed just above and I could almost touch them. Earth was so close that I felt the grass growing under my feet. I stood looking up for a long time. Long enough to perceive the earth rotate against the stars. Now and then a shooting star raced across the blackness.

What if I pushed with my feet? I wondered. Could I make the earth turn faster? Or if I pushed the other way, could I slow it down? I planted my feet for a better grip and lurched hard to the West, forcing the earth to move a little faster to the East. It seemed to budge ever so little against the stars!

"How much power it takes!" I exclaimed. If there is a God, I thought, how much power God must have to set all this in motion. And how much wisdom to know all the stars and each blade of grass. And if God *cares* about me, how fortunate I am.

On the other hand, if there is no God, how sobering to live in this swirl of forces and have no recourse if they crush me. What if I am just another shooting star that flashes for a moment and falls unnoticed in the field over there?

How important that God cares, I thought. If God has an interest in me, then life has a meaning no matter what else happens, no matter how ineffectual my effort to move the world. I went indoors thinking that something of me will endure forever. My very self will be treasured in God's eternal heart.

To Be Loved by Anyone at All

Sometimes the gift of being known and loved is the only possible meaning in an otherwise cruel and colorless world.

The psychologist, Dr. Viktor Frankl was number 119,104 at Auschwitz. He spent most of World War II in slavery digging railroad tracks. Like other imprisoned Jews, he was subjected to arbitrary beatings and starvation. In spite of these conditions, he found ways to deepen his spiritual life. One way was to think about loved ones who might care. In his book, *Man's Search for Meaning*, he describes one morning when the prisoners were marching out to work.

> We stumbled on in the darkness, over big stones and through large puddles, along the one road leading from the camp. The accompanying guards kept shouting at us and driving us with the butts of their rifles. Anyone with very sore feet supported himself on his neighbor's arm. Hardly a word was spoken; the icy wind did not encourage talk. Hiding his mouth behind his upturned collar, the man marching next to me whispered suddenly, "If our wives could see us now! I do hope they are better off in their camps and don't know what is happening to us." ...
>
> "Stop!" We had arrived at the work site. Everybody rushed into the dark hut in the hope of getting a fairly decent tool. Each prisoner got a spade or a pickax.
>
> "Can't you hurry up, you pigs?" Soon we had resumed the previous day's positions in the ditch. The frozen ground cracked under the point of the pickaxes, the sparks flew. The men were silent, their brains numb. My mind still clung to the image of my wife...
>
> The guard passed by, insulting me, and once again I communed with my beloved. More and more I felt that she was present, that she was with me; I had the feeling that I was able to touch her, able to stretch out my hand and grasp hers. The feeling was very strong: she was there. Then, at that very moment, a bird flew down silently and perched just in front of me, on the heap of soil which I had dug up from the ditch, and looked steadily at me.

V. Frankl, Man's Search for Meaning,
NY, Pocket, 1963, pp.57ff. Abridged.

To Be Honored By a Great Man

Forty years after Dr. Frankl's imprisonment, my friend Tony had this odd, contrasting experience. It, too, is a story of being cared about, though with a strange twist. Tony was on a flight from Albuquerque to Minneapolis. He sat next to an older, foreign-looking man. The man's clothes had that tweedy European look. Sure enough, when the flight attendant asked what he wanted to drink, the man had trouble with English and said, "Orangensaft." Tony had worked for several years in Germany, so he asked in German if he could help.

"Yes, please," said the man. "Tell him I'd like some orange juice." And so they fell into conversation. The man talked a lot about the airplane, its maneuvers and technicalities. He remarked about the construction of the ailerons.

"You seem to know a lot about airplanes," said Tony.

"Yes, I am a pilot. I have been with Lufthansa for many years. And I flew before that too. In fact, I used to fly fighter planes in the Wehrmacht."

"Really? You were in World War II?"

"Oh yes, but I am sorry about that now. I was a pilot but not a Nazi. The damned Nazis made it bad for all of us, you know."

"That's true," replied Tony.

"My mother was French," the man went on. "So I was not allowed to be a Nazi. Also I didn't care for their ideals."

"Hitler certainly had some strange ideas about the world and who should be in it."

"Oh, it wasn't Hitler," said the German. "It was the Nazis."

26

Tony furrowed his brow. "I'm afraid I don't follow you. Who were the Nazis if not Hitler?"

"Let me tell you, my young friend, that most people do not know the real Hitler. Goebbles, Goering, Hess and those people were the bad apples. Hitler was really a very nice man."

"How can you say that?" Tony challenged.

"When I was a young pilot—I was the youngest in the squadron—we were flying the new BF109's. This was in 1935 and the Messerschmidt was an experimental airplane. One day our squadron leader told us to fly cover for a group of civilian aircraft. It was a nice day and we enjoyed the flight. It was easy to keep the three large planes in view. Finally, the squadron leader radioed us to land.

"When we climbed out of our cockpits, he was very excited and ordered us to stand at attention in front of our planes. Soon the passenger planes landed, and out stepped the most important men in the country, including the Fuehrer. When Hitler saw us, he walked over to our squadron where we were in line by order of rank. The squadron leader puffed out his chest and waited for the Fuehrer to speak. But he walked right past the squadron leader. He walked past the senior pilots. He spoke only to the youngest—to me.

'Well, Leutnant,' he asked. 'What do you think of the 109?'

'It's a wonderful plane, sir.'

'Does it handle well?'

'Ja wohl, Mein Fuehrer. It is very smooth and maneuverable. The best I have ever flown!'

'Do you think it will give you an advantage in a dog fight?'

'Absolutely,' I said. 'It is very fast. The nose cannon is highly accurate and the machine guns are excellent.'

"He seemed satisfied, clicked his heels in a little dance and started to turn away. But he suddenly stopped and came back. He asked me, 'And what do you think of the food? Is it adequate? Does it taste good?'"

"I wasn't quite sure what to say since everyone was listening and I was the youngest. But I said, 'It is quite adequate. Yes sir, it tastes excellent.'"

'Come, come,' he chided me, 'there must be something. Spit it out.'

'With all due respect,' I replied, 'they only serve coffee in my squadron mess. It is very *good* coffee. But I prefer cocoa.'

'Damn,' said Hitler, 'they should serve coffee *and* cocoa at every meal.' And with that, he marched over to the squadron leader and scolded him about the meals. He cared for us, you see."

It's Who You Know That Counts

It's not just that we love, but who loves us back. In this form of meaning to really be alive is to be known, and not just by anyone. When I told this story to Dave he thought it was stupid to value Hitler's love. "Who cares," he asked, "if Hitler loved anyone?" I had to agree, Hitler was a terrible person, but he was in a position to bestow recognition. Some people care about things like that. My father-in-law, for example, proudly talked about the time he shook hands with Chicago's Mayor Daley. It was a highlight for him. His motto was: "It's not what you know but who you know that counts." Of course, he meant: it's who knows you.

Questions for Reflection

Has any famous or important person shown regard for you?
How has that affected you?

Does someone special love you? How important is that love?

Do you believe that some eternal person always cares about
you no matter what?

Oh, Daddy, it's so good to have a penny in your pocket.

Young girl

ENJOYING BEAUTY AND TREASURE

Moving along in the Realm of Having, we enter a great marketplace. It's filled with shops of every sort: large stores stuffed with discount items, expensive boutiques, art galleries, street vendors with carts, and blankets on the sidewalk displaying turquoise jewelry. This is where people find meaning in having a relationship with things of value.

I Always Wanted One of These

"Let's go shopping in Mexico," Kay proposed. It was the third day of my family's visit with her in Texas, and it was time to get out of the house. "I don't know," I said, "I'm not much of a shopper; I'd rather go to the rodeo." "Oh, c'mon," she insisted, "we'll go to the rodeo tomorrow." Everyone else thought shopping would be fun, so we jumped into her Cadillac and drove off to Matamoros.

The town was a dense warren of shops, stalls, carts and hawkers. The special bargains were wool blankets, leather purses, onyx statuary and cotton dresses. "We shouldn't buy too much," I cautioned, "since we have no extra space in our luggage." But Kay was a dedicated shopper and took us to the best places anyway. We bought a belt for myself and a purse for Maureen. "These things are small and we really need them," I said. This satisfied my practical interest, and I was ready to go sample tequila.

31

"What about this, Hon?" Maureen asked, looking at a marble statue. "Don't you think it would be nice for your mother?"

"It's nice," I said, "but isn't it a little heavy to take on the airplane?"

"Don't worry," she replied, "I think we can fit it in Annie's bag." This didn't track logically, but I let it go. I could tell she just wanted to buy it.

We spent the afternoon looking at beautiful merchandise, thinking about each family member and weighing the tonnage of our acquisitions. The magic words that melted my reluctance were: "Wouldn't this be nice for So-and-So?" The expression, "You know, I've always wanted one of these" had its effect too.

By the end of the day, we filled Kay's trunk with a marble statue, an onyx chess set, a china soup tureen, two bottles of Kalua, a quart of vanilla, a bag of folding goods, a bronze tree with black birds, two cowboy hats, and assorted boots, wallets, purses and belts. It was like the twelve days of Christmas. And to top it all off, a huge piñata horse for Annie's next birthday. Everyone was thrilled with the treasures. Even I, the shopping grinch, had to admit that we made a good haul. Kay was ecstatic. Getting nice things is important to her.

Buy That—It's You

Kay is someone who finds special meaning in beautiful things. People like her believe that humanity expresses itself best in art and treasure. The decor you choose for your room, they think, says something about who you are and how you relate to others. What you gather around you is an extension of yourself. Tools give you a sense of power. Souvenirs remind you of treasured events. Gifts make a statement to cherished friends. Each piece is a sacrament of personal meaning. "Buy that," Kay said, "it's really you."

The Community Treasure

Sometimes the meaning embodied in possessions is not strictly personal; it comes from something larger—from your community or culture.

Agnes and Cecile are two sisters I befriended among the millions of French families who camp on the Mediterranean beach every August. I liked them because they were vivacious and got things going—like volley ball games. They lived with their parents in the French Alpine town of Annecy where they both taught school. I visited them four or five times during my studies, usually for skiing trips. After an absence of fourteen years, I went back with my wife on a business trip. The sisters still lived in the same building, though now they shared an apartment across the hall from their parents. The furnishings were modest, embellished only with throw sheets and cushions.

In the evening they drove us around town in a flat-sided "Deux Chevaux" like the one we took skiing years before. We saw the lake, the castle and all the local churches. My rusty French strained on words like "girder, parapet, and flying buttress." "Why," challenged Agnes, "are your translations for your wife so much shorter than my explanations?"

The last stop on the tour was their parish church, St. Etienne's. They took us from front to back and pointed out every detail with growing enthusiasm. They knew where the light switches were and had the keys to every door. In the baptistery we heard how the founding pastor had acquired the carved stone basin. In the loft they showed us the sixteenth century organ that Cecile played every fourth Sunday. In the bell tower we saw the clock that their father, a retired mechanic, kept in repair. Then into the sacristy. They pulled open every drawer to show vestments which their sewing group had made. They threw open the cabinets to show a vast collection of shining ecclesiastical objects—censors, relics, ciboria, chalices, monstrances—that the parish had acquired from all the ancient churches in the province of Haute Savoie.

When all the doors were open and all the treasures laid bare, their eyes sparkled with excitement. This was *their* church, they were the sacristans, and these were their treasures. Though not in their personal names, they *owned* these beautiful things. This property, gathered from the territory around, embodied the sacred values of the community into which they poured their tireless energy. We felt honored to be shown these cup-boarded objects, not only because they were beautiful, but because to appreciate them was to share the patrimony of the larger community.

Annie's Collections

Collectors are the true fans of the meaning in things. I know because I live with one.

My daughter Annie has a lot of "junk" in her room. Sometimes she dutifully cleans it up, but even then it's hard to navigate around all the stuff. None of it has monetary value. Some of it is just rocks. But these are her treasures. She has two major collections: her stuffed animals and her baseball cards. The animals are partly collection and partly friends. She takes one or two to bed with her every night.

I don't know why she collects baseball cards. She got interested because her brother, Joey, started a collection when all the other boys were doing it. So she had to start one too, just to be fair. But he got tired of them. Joey is not a collector. He is always looking for the next better thing. So Annie inherited his box-full. For her, possession is a value in itself. A treasure. While he schemes to get a motor for his bike, she sits for hours sorting her cards into piles—by color, by team, by statistics. To her the cards have value worth reviewing again and again.

The Button Convention

Then there are the adult collectors. Their passion reaches to a public cult. Recently the annual convention of the International Society of Button Collectors was held in our city auditorium. It drew a crowd of thousands from around the world. The Society was founded during the Great Depression to provide an inexpensive outlet for unemployed collectors. Anyone could save a few buttons from an old shirt. Now their descendants display millions of buttons varying in value from a few pennies to hundreds of dollars. There were buttons from the 18th century, the Victorian period and modern times. Some were hand-made; others mass-produced. They were fashioned from every material: wood, plastic, fiber, fabric, brass, bone and silver. There were plain ones and fancy ones. Men's buttons and women's buttons. Some in sets on cards and others alone in jewelry cases.

The conventioneers talked excitedly about the significance of buttons: their technology, utility, and contribution to human well-being. One man said, "Without buttons you'd have to squirm into your clothes or tie them on like barbarians." Others were impressed with buttons as an art form. "Art in miniature" was in fact the theme of the convention. Every art form was represented: painting, engraving, molding, sculpting, stitching, weaving and printing. Some people focused on historical value. "These," said one lady, "were made by a partisan of Andrew Jackson. His name was secretly engraved on the back so that the wearer unwittingly supported Jackson for president."

Buttons, dolls and baseball cards are not exactly the Holy Grail, but to those who collect them, they represent a world of meaning. This world is personal, intelligible, filled with value and greater than self. It engages the collector in an enduring purpose. One man who left his own stall to browse the others, explained it this way: "It's an eternal quest," he said, "I never get tired of it."

A Real Thing

An Ethiopian boy helped me understand what people are looking for in these things. Salamon was the son of the hotel keeper where I was staying in Bahir Dar. He directed me to the sites around Lake Tana. In the evening he showed me his books and let me read one on the history of his country. By local standards he was not poor. He had a wristwatch. Everywhere else in this isolated fishing village manufactured goods were so scarce that my empty tin cans were good for three eggs. I thanked him with time and English lessons, the two things I had to share. But Salamon said he wanted something more. He wanted a "thing."

"Salamon, what kind of thing do you want?"

"A *real* thing," he replied, surveying the contents of my backpack spread out on the table. "Something you brought with you from America. Something like your knife."

"I am on a long journey. I need my knife every day."

"How about something else from your pack, like your first aid kit?" He picked it up and turned it before his eyes.

"I need all the things in my pack for the journey. What if I get sick and need some medicine?" We stood in silence for a long time, the negotiations at full stop. "How about this?" I said at last. "It's an American dime."

"I don't want money."

"I know, but it's the one thing in my pack that I don't need every day."

He thought for a while. And then accepting it he said, "It's not a real thing, but at least it was made in America."

I don't know what makes something real or valuable. Sometimes its beauty, rarity, the place it comes from, who touched it before, or what it can be used for. But when we human beings find a "real thing," we treasure it.

Questions for Reflection

What do you especially treasure? Why is it valuable to you?

What do the things you own say about who you are?

How do your possessions enlarge your sense of meaning?

*There is a time for
everything under
heaven.*

Qoheleth

GETTING YOUR FAIR SHARE

We come next to the Great Square of Justice. It's another huge plaza in the realm of Having. It is filled with people and surrounded by massive buildings. On one side we see the courthouse, the legislature, and the jail. These are the symbols of human justice. Human justice is defined in law and meted out case by case. Around the other sides of the square we see the cathedral, the casino and the tents of many fortune tellers. These are the symbols of *philosophical* justice. Philosophical justice is defined by getting your fair share out of life. It's not just about having this or that. It's about having *enough*.

Who Cleans Up the Yard?

It was the last day of school and we celebrated with meatloaf and mashed potatoes (a family favorite). When we sat down I told the kids, "Mom and I want to talk about the summer schedule. We already know about camp, swimming lessons and stuff like that. So let's talk about bedtime."

"Good," said Joey. "I like summer because we can stay up later."

"That's true," replied Mom, "but this summer we want you on a regular schedule. No more just going to bed and getting up when you want. That didn't work last summer. I never got any rest."

Annie is always the first to defend herself. "Well, I don't think we should have to get up before eight in the morning. Can I have some more meatloaf?"

"Wait till everyone is at least halfway done with their firsts," I admonished. "Eight in the morning sounds reasonable to me. I also think bedtime should be extended from nine to nine-thirty." Annie's eyes lit up with that.

"What's important to me," said Mom, "is that the kids are in their rooms by nine o'clock so I don't have to be on duty all night."

"That makes sense," said Annie. "What's taking you all so long with your firsts?"

"I think I should stay up later than her," said Joey. "After all, I'm eleven and she's only nine." The parents agreed that he was the older and should stay up later. We had mistakenly neglected this birth-right, and now would be a good time to remedy our fault. He could stay up till ten.

"Okay," concluded Mom, "as long as you are responsible for your own bedtime business and turn out your own light."

While we negotiated with Joey about his extra time and responsibility, Annie's face became more and more distressed. Finally she stomped out of the kitchen leaving a big slab of second helping on her plate. "You don't even care if I exist!" she spat out as she marched by my chair.

About five minutes later, after Joey left the table, she returned and repeated her assessment: "You don't care about me at all!"

"Are you upset because Joey is going to stay up later than you?"

"Yes! We always go to bed at the same time."

"But we realize that was a mistake. We have to start giving Joey privileges according to his being older and more responsible. It's what families do."

"But I'm responsible. I do everything you ask. Lots of times more than he does."

"Ohhh, Annie," said Mom. "You're such a good girl. Of course you do. And you do so much to help your brother when he can't hear things." (Joey wears hearing aids.) By this time Annie was in Mom's lap weeping.

We continued to acknowledge her grown-up-ness and at the same time to explain about his being older, and how we were trying to help Joey understand his growing responsibility.

"Well, if he's so responsible," she accused, "how come he doesn't have to do more?"

"I think you're on to something, Annie." The light came on in my mind. "In fact, you're absolutely right. If he's older and more responsible, then he should have more jobs with his privileges. How about if on Saturdays he has to pick three jobs from the list and you have to pick only two?"

"Well...," she thought about it for a moment. "Okay, but he has to be the only one who picks up the dog poop in the yard!"

"It's a deal," we said. So with her sense of justice assuaged, she jumped up off Mom's lap and went out to skip rope on the front sidewalk.

Fairness as a Meaning of Life

All children, like Annie, feel keenly the meaningfulness of justice. In youth we argue passionately about "what's mine", "what's fair" and "what's not fair." After many experiences of getting more and getting less, we form an impression about the general "fairness" of life. We might even sum up our whole philosophy around this idea.

My frequent flyer account says that I have flown over 120,000 miles on just one airline. You'd think I'd be used to take-offs and landings by now. In many ways I am, since I no longer listen to what the flight attendant says about FAA regulations or escape hatches. But as soon as the plane turns down the runway and the engines thunder, I always close my book and fold my hands in my lap. It's been a good life, I say to myself. If the plane goes down—well, I've had my fair share of everything.

God's Role in Distributing Justice

In searching for this kind of meaning many people look to God. Whenever we receive an extraordinary boon—we get a thousand dollars we didn't expect, troublesome neighbors move away, or the doctor says our tumor is benign—do we not turn our eyes to heaven and say, "Thank you, thank you, thank you"? And when something really bad happens—our business fails, a friend deserts us, or our child dies in an accident—do we not also turn to heaven and ask, "Why me?" What did I do to deserve this? Why not spread this evil around a little better?"

We turn to God because God is supposed to be so powerful and wise. If we can't control what life gives us, then maybe we can find the meaning of it in divine providence. If only we could see it as part of a *plan*. And surely, if it was God's plan, it would be fair—mysterious perhaps, but surely fair.

Belief in this kind of plan makes it easier to accept an unusual amount of misfortune. There are different theories about this. Some think that extra misfortune is a perverse consequence of original sin. Some say it's a test. Others say that it's a proof of God's grace. Still others believe that it is an extra share in the passion of the Lord.

The Great Bungler in the Sky

Or maybe the plan isn't a real plan after all but more of a prank. Maybe he does it just for the "hell" of it. As Tevye says in *Fiddler on the Roof*: "Sometimes when things are too quiet up there you say, 'Let's see what mischief I can play on my friend, Tevye.'"

One night a group of us fell into dispute about these divine intentions. One woman started it by hinting at her husband Ned's shady past.

Ned is a massive, burly guy who grew up in a tough North side neighborhood. Fifteen years ago he stabbed a man in a bar fight. Even today he has a bald greaser look. If he wasn't already a friend of mine, I sure wouldn't want to meet him in a dark alley. But he has a pretty good sense of humor, and he had the prudence to marry a policeman's daughter and take up auto mechanics.

"Sure I killed a guy," said Ned. "What's that got to do with anything?"

"Well," she clarified, "don't you think that maybe God ..."

"That God is punishing me with a handicapped child? Nuts! I already paid for that with seven years in the joint."

This night we were at a Special Ed support group, and the subject of the injustice of our kids' handicaps came up. Nobody felt they deserved this kind of jolt.

"Don't look at me," said Ned. "I done worse than all of you, and it happened to you too."

"Well, look at it this way," said someone, "at least it will make better persons of us."

"I can live without being re-made into a better person," said someone else.

"Why do we have to say there's any justice in it?" asked Ned. "Why don't we just say God is a bungler who screwed up? Then at least we'd know who to be mad at."

Later I grabbed Ned and led him off behind the portable blackboard. "You know," I said, "I've always been a pretty religious person, but I agree with you. Since this happened to my kid, I've called God every name in the book." We compared names, and some of them were pretty awful. No lightning struck, and we began to laugh.

If God is the great administrator of justice, then sometimes all you can do is laugh to accept his plan.

Karma—The Moral Vending Machine

Some people find the answer to life's fairness in other explanations. We see their ideas symbolized by the large number of booths of fortune tellers, palm readers and soothsayers in the middle of the Square. Next to the fountain is a device that looks like a vending machine.

This machine represents what many call Karma. Karma is the belief that some impartial, cosmic law requires a fair exchange of good and evil. The law says: If you do good you will receive good; if you do evil you will receive evil. It's that simple.

Karma has wide acceptance in many cultures and belief systems. It goes by different names: Karma, justice, merit, purgatory, atonement, and the law of cause and effect.

Karma in Kathmandu

One day when I was studying in Kathmandu, Nepal, I visited the Badhnath stupa, a great white dome topped by a square tower. Each side of the tower was painted with a huge eye. The eyes inspected the doings of human beings in every direction. Across the street, I was told, was the home of the Chini-lama, the third ranking Buddhist monk in the world. The house was modest but clean and substantial. A cream-colored Mercedes-Benz was parked out front. I gathered my courage and entered the courtyard. A woman guessed my purpose and ushered me to the second floor where I met an old man sitting on a divan. He said he was the lama and that he would talk with me. I took this as a unique opportunity to talk with a world leader about how his community is organized, administered, and governed. I figured I could ask any learned person about Buddhist doctrine. But this man could give me first-hand information about the politics of it all.

To my surprise he said very little about the practical issues of government. Instead, he made constant reference to the law of Karma. "There is no involvement," he said, "of Buddhism in politics. If we leave them alone, they leave us alone. There is no sense remonstrating with a bad ruler. A good ruler shall rule long; a bad ruler, short." On the subject of business he said, "If a man is right-living, he will succeed in business." He then proceeded to demonstrate how he meditates and pointed out that he had no need of material things—no need to look at his wrist watch or to listen to his transistor radio which was on a shelf nearby. "I am a right-living man," he said. To prove how Karma worked for him he opened his mouth and said, "Look, 83 years old and perfect teeth." Except for a few gold fillings, he was right.

I tell this story not to demean my host, who was after all conversing with a stranger in a foreign tongue, but only to point out how all-pervasive was the law of Karma in his thinking. It gave meaning to every topic.

Many people live by their own law of Karma. It has a powerful effect on their sense of fairness and brings them to conclusions like the following:

- "I cannot die until I have atoned for my sins."
- "At retirement I will finally reap the benefit of all my toil."
- "The wrongs I have suffered will someday be avenged."
- "She was such a good person, surely she has gone to her reward."

A Formula for Good and Evil

Some people believe that *fate* controls the fairness of life. Things just are the way they are. It helps, however, to know the formula that fate uses.

My friend Bridgette has a mathematical formula for calculating the fairness of life. "The way I see it," she says, "life has a four-to-one ratio of good to evil. For every four good days there will be one bad day, or a particular event will be four parts good and one part bad."

She feels satisfied that life is meaningful as long as the ratio stays relatively constant. "What makes me uncomfortable," she says, "is when the balance goes too far in either direction. If I get too much good in a row, lets say six, seven or eight, then there's bound to be a disaster."

"What about the other way?" I asked.

"That too. Three or four evils in a row and your luck has to swing the other way. But when it goes to five or six, that's when the system breaks down because it would take too much good to make up for this much evil. That much good is hardly possible."

And so it goes with astrology, biorhythms, Murphy's Law, the 80/20 rule, and hundreds of aphorisms like:

- "Into every life some rain must fall."
- "It was too good to be true."
- "Every cloud has a silver lining."
- "I've got good news and bad news."

They all express a formula for anticipating a scheduled amount of good and evil in life. And the meaning of it all derives from the assumed "fact" that the balance of good and evil was at least predictable and sufficient—if not entirely "fair."

Finding Your Formula

Some people get discouraged about the degree of injustice in the world and in their own lives. They can't believe in a god who lets terrible things happen and find it hard to accept their lot. They are not the ones who find meaning in this sense of fairness. Perhaps they find solace in the fact that justice is not the only form of meaning.

Others perceive a deep meaning here. If you are one of them, I hope that you find the formula that satisfies your philosophical sense of justice, so that, like Annie, you too can go out and jump rope, content that what you have is enough.

Questions for Reflection

How much of life's good things do you expect to get? Have you had your fair share?

What controls how much good and bad fortune you receive?

What will you do if you don't get enough?

Who among your friends or relatives cares deeply about this sense of meaning?

---

*A place for
everything and
everything in its
place.*

A proverb

HAVING A SENSE OF ORDER

Our last stop in the Realm of Having is a middle-class neighborhood where everything is neat, cultivated and smells of soap. This is the place of order, the home of those who find meaning in having the world imbued with perfection, cleanliness and rationality.

Entering here reminds me of the first time I crossed from France into Germany. Right from the border I could see a difference. The German hedges were trimmed; the roads were curbed; the houses squared-off and painted. In sharp contrast, the French houses were cement gray; the roads, haphazard; and the hedges—well, let's just say they were self-expressive.

Order prevails in Germany, more than anywhere else in the world. I once tried to cross a street in Tuebingen against a red light. People shouted me back even though no traffic was coming. What surprised me was their unanimous belief in the value of following rules. It wasn't something that just a few people did, but something they all held sacred. This kind of order belongs to the realm of Having. It's a relationship to the world—an appreciation of the rational quality that all things have, or should have.

Order of this type appeals to the mind. As Paul Claudel says, "Order is the joy of reason." Everybody (Claudel was a Frenchman!) appreciates a measure of social order and predictability, but some people are highly attracted to it. They want it not only for themselves but for the world as a whole. The more order, they feel, the better—the greater the sense of meaning.

A Heroine of Social Order

Frau Beuchler was my landlady in Tuebingen. Her house was a shrine to what Herman Hesse calls "superhuman housewifery." Her life ran on a strict schedule. And her family was exceedingly well-groomed.

One day she stopped me going out the back door. "Herr Kramlinger, please be sure to clean the bathtub when you finish washing."

"Yes, thank you. I will," I said as I continued on my way. It was a reasonable request, I thought, but also strange because I always scrubbed the ring out of the tub. My mother had taught me that much, and more.

Frau Beuchler repeated her request several times. Each time I grew more puzzled and irritated. Then she mentioned it again. "How much cleaner can I make it?" I asked, suppressing an urge to snarl.

"Come, I'll show you," she said. "There, see!" She pointed to dried water spots on the metal spout. She didn't want me to just clean the tub. She wanted me to polish the fixtures. Now that's perfection beyond my understanding!

It is easy to poke fun at people like Frau Beuchler. They often focus on the little things, so that we call them "petty." The order they try so mightily to maintain is fragile. It is easily challenged by the forces of change like wind, frost, tree roots, weeds and human impulse. Even the quiet indoor air drops lint on their perfect arrangements.

Yet we should not discount their insight. There *is* meaning in order. Without the order of natural law, the planets would fly apart. Without social order we would have to fight each other for the smallest things, even for our lives. Keeping the rules is a way to participate in this great but fragile relationship with the world. It contributes to the good of one's fellows by confirming the basic covenant of society. The great lawgivers from Hammurabi to Jefferson were heroes of this kind of meaning. So was Frau Beuchler. Sweeping the sidewalk and polishing the bath fixtures was her way to keep the planets in their orbits. On Frau Beuchler's headstone I would write: "She kept the world peaceful and orderly for all to enjoy."

A Convert to Order

I said that my mother taught me a lot about order. In her house an ash tray was a decoration, and a wastebasket a place to store toys. If you wanted to throw something away you had to use the *real* wastebasket under the sink in the kitchen. My brother never liked this regime and tried to keep things as messy as possible. He was the rebel in our house, a fugitive from order. He left home as soon as possible after high school and became a social worker. Perhaps he intended to remake the world according to a higher principle for the sake of the unclean and the outcast. Yet in time he too converted back to a more domestic sense of order.

A few years ago I visited him in the old house he had carefully remodeled. We were getting ready to go to a family celebration. We knew our mother would be there.

"One thing that always bugged me about Mom," he said, "was how much she wanted to control our lives. It was impossible to live a normal life with all her rules about cleaning the house. All she cared about was order, perfection and punctuality."

Then, without thinking, he bent over and picked a piece of lint off the floor and discarded it in the wastebasket under the sink in the kitchen. "C'mon," he said, "or we'll be late."

A Gold Medal Winner

Here's a story that shows how close the pursuit of order has got to me.

One morning during the summer Olympic Games my family was sitting around the breakfast table. We had been watching the games for several evenings on television. We saw Russian gymnasts score perfect 10's. American divers scored 9.99 and 9.98. Gold medals had been won by only a few hundredths, even thousandths of a point.

On this morning the subject of the children's behavior came up—how well they were doing their chores around the house.

"Let's say we had a Household Olympics," I suggested. "What scores do you think you would get? Do you think you would get a gold medal for making your bed?"

"That's the trouble with you, Dad," said Annie, "you expect a perfect ten on every event."

"No, I don't."

"Well, then a 9.9," she shot back.

Mom picked up the idea and said, "What *would* be a good score around here?"

"Eight," said Joey.

"Maybe 8.5", said Annie.

"How about 8.59?" I urged.

"There you go again, Dad," complained Annie. "You're always trying to squeeze out some extra perfection."

We settled on 8.3 as a family standard and turned our attention back to breakfast.

"I hate to tell you this, Dad," said Annie, "but the eggs are only a 7.5."

"Would you go for 7.59?"

"Daaaaad!"

Questions for Reflection

How important is order for your sense of well-being?

What rules do you depend on to stay the same in life?

How do you feel when your surroundings are messy and disorganized?

What role do you play in promoting order in the world?

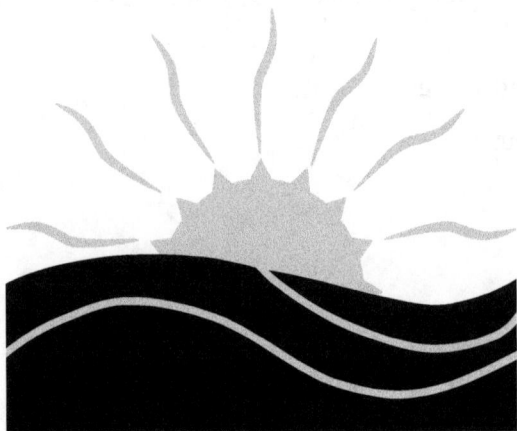

THE REALM OF DOING

See here where the road turns sharply upward? This is where we depart from the fertile lowlands of Having and begin the uphill journey into the Realm of Doing. This is the second of three vast domains in which people find meaning. Plato, likens Doing to the muscular torso of the human body, because it is the place of effort, strength and achievement. This is where people acquire meaning in deliberate personal action.

In the Realm of Having, the meaning of life flows primarily from the outside in—from the beloved, from treasures, from order in the world. The meaning lies there in rich abundance to be plucked and harvested through relationships. In the Realm of Doing, however, the flow reverses. People here do not so much find meaning as *create* it. They create it from the inside out by their own purposeful behavior. If they don't like the meaning they see, they change it.

The Realm of Doing is spare compared to the Realm of Having. Yes, there are plenty of material things, but they are tools rather than treasures. There are more desks to work at than benches to sit on. Yet there is excitement in the air—lots of vitality, drama, decision-making and action.

The road we will follow leads first through a business district populated by energetic figures in uniforms and business suits. Further along is new construction where workers advance the cause of civilization. Then the road cuts through snow-capped mountains to the land of high adventure where fewer people travel--usually alone, lightly equipped and alert to danger.

Finally, the road rises to an impressive town on the high ground of moral action. Its streets glitter with temptation, but the people steadfastly follow a beacon of righteousness shining from the highest spire.

If you're ready for this invigorating part of our journey, let's begin.

There is nothing so inspiring as the sight of a legitimate ambition.

Theodore Dreiser

ACHIEVING A GREAT GOAL

Achievement is the first and most popular source of meaning in the domain of personal action. Its adherents find meaning in the excellence of what they create and accomplish. As Robert Fritz says, "Creating is the place where the human spirit shines its greatest light."

Mom and Dad start it off. "Oh, look what Bobby can do!" they say. Bobby's own excitement, especially if Bobby is a first child, can lead to a life in which achievement is the dominant theme. The next steps are good report cards, a band recital, and merit badges. Then high school diplomas, honorable discharges, a master's degree, a citizen's award—even a bowling trophy.

Achievement at Work

The most common arena for achievement is the world of work or business. Only a few of us can win the Indy 500 or a Nobel Prize. But we can all find a niche in the economy. The world of work is organized around achievement—around producing results for which someone is willing to pay.

This sense of meaning is so common that many people answer the question, "Who are you?" by stating the title of their job.

Ruth is a good example. She started her career as a secretary. Then she became an administrative assistant. She did excellent work, but always supporting someone else's success. Not prepared to start her own business or sponsor a novel project, she gradually worked her way from one administrative post to another—each time acquiring just a little more experience and responsibility.

One day the department exploded around her. The executive in charge resigned. The creative genius behind the department's new product was given the boot. And the product itself was downgraded from pampered project to excess inventory. In the chaos Ruth volunteered to manage the sale of the product. Here was her chance to achieve something real. She couldn't have invented the product, but she could make it succeed in the marketplace. She poured her energy into meeting clients and pumping up sales people. She organized the remaining employees into application specialists and focused them on customer needs. Few in the organization called her a great manager or leader. But she made the product a success. From her point of view, it was worth all the pain. She had achieved what would normally have been beyond her.

Almost His Own Company

Doug is another achiever. I met him because our children went to the same school. He works for a major utility, and friends there tell me he is one of their "corporate heroes." Doug not only wants to achieve personal success; he expects everyone else to achieve as well. For example, when many of us parents were not satisfied with a teacher at the school, Doug challenged the administrator. "What are your standards of performance?" he asked at a parent meeting, "Who supervises this teacher? You? What are you doing to improve her performance?" The poor administrator squirmed uncomfortably, because improving performance was not his highest priority. His idea of a good day was when everyone showed up and someone brought cookies to the staff meeting.

Doug left the utility to start his own company. During this time he studied business management at Harvard. To manage his own business successfully and with excellence—that was the ultimate achievement.

Achievement as Completion

Achievement can be more than getting business results. For some, it's a matter of just completing something they set out to do.

Nancy studied piano as a child. She practiced every day for the great recital in the school auditorium. She picked out two pieces and practiced until she could play them with her eyes closed. On the great day she put on a new pink dress with ruffles. She waited through 13 other recitals. Finally, it was her turn. The first piece went fine—only one sour note. Midway through the second piece she lost her way and couldn't remember the rest of the music. She froze and then fled from the stage.

Her teacher tried to rebuild her confidence. "You can do it, Nancy," she said. "Here, take your music and go finish the recital." Nancy wasn't sure, so they sent out the next boy on the program. "Listen," said the teacher, "we can put you on next or at the end of the program. Take the music with you. I know you can do it."

In the meantime, Nancy's mother came backstage. Trying to console, she said, "It's not that important, Nancy. If you don't feel up to it, you don't have to go back out there." Nancy hesitated for a minute, looking back and forth from her mother to her teacher. Finally she went to her mother and decided not to finish the recital.

The music went back on the piano at home. She didn't play it any more so it got moved to the box under the bench. Eventually, it made its way to the attic. Nancy got over the hurt, and moved on to many adult accomplishments: children, poetry, years of teaching. Still, the memory haunted her and reminded her of her limitations.

One day while cleaning out her mother's attic she found the old music books. There were the pieces she had marked for the great recital. What would happen, she thought, if I could go back and finish it? How different would my life be?

So she bought another pink dress with ruffles, invited some friends to a party and finished the recital. Her friends never guessed why she had to play those juvenile pieces. But inside she beamed with the pride of accomplishment.

The Peachseed Monkey

One of my favorite stories about completion comes from Sam Keen's book, *To a Dancing God*:

> One endless summer afternoon when I was a boy my father sat in the eternal shade of a peach tree, carving on a seed he had picked up. With increasing excitement and covetousness, I watched while, using a skill common to all omnipotent creators, he fashioned a small monkey out of the seed. If only I could have it. Finally, I marshaled my nerve and asked if I might have the monkey when it was finished. My father replied, "This one is for your mother, but I will carve you one someday."
>
> Days passed, and then weeks and, finally, years, and the someday on which I was to receive the monkey did not arrive. In truth, I forgot all about the peach-seed monkey.

Years later with emphysema sapping his energy, my father and I sat under a juniper tree. I listened as he wrestled with the task of taking the measure of his success and failure in life. There came a moment of silence that cried out for testimony. Suddenly I remembered the peach-seed monkey, and I heard the right words coming from myself to fill the silence: "In all that is important you have never failed me. With one exception, you kept the promises you made to me—you never carved me that peach-seed monkey."

Not long after this conversation I received a small package in the mail. In it was a peach-seed monkey and a note which said: "Here is the monkey I promised you. You will notice that I broke one leg and had to repair it with glue. I am sorry I didn't have time to carve a perfect one."

Two weeks later my father died. He died only at the end of his life.

Sam Keen, To a Dancing God, *NY, Harper and Row, 1970, p. 100f. Edited.*

I Can Do Anything

Sometimes the meaning of achievement comes as a feeling of competence or responsibility. A young lady named Ann H. told me this story about her experience.

"Ann, this has got to stop! You're 20 years old and not getting anywhere. And now this. A tattoo! Of all things!"

"Mo-om," she replied, "Nobody can see it. Besides, it's nice. A butterfly and a rose..."

"It's not nice!" Mother stopped for a moment, and the energy drained from her voice. "Oh, Ann, when are you going to settle down? You're crazy, you know? Always one party after another. When are you going to finish something?"

Ann said nothing more but thought about the conversation for a long while. She's right, she admitted to herself. I've started more projects than I've finished. Well, I almost finished crocheting those mittens. So, why don't I just finish them?

I don't know, she answered her own question, I guess anyone can do mittens. At least any girl can. What I should really do is fix up a car. Then people would take notice. She paused in her thoughts. And as for parties, what the heck, I like them. I'm working. And as long as I have the money and my car works, why not?

This all happened in early October. On the way to a Halloween party her '78 Camaro stopped with an ear-grinding clank.

"Cracked block," said her boyfriend.

"Fourteen hundred minimum," said the neighbor across the street.

"I guess this means you're grounded, Hon," said her father. "We've just paid two thousand dollars for your braces and neither you nor we have the money for another car."

"But a new block is only two hundred fifty," she said.

"Yeah, but who is going to do the work?"

"I am," she said resolutely. "It's my car and my responsibility. And I'm going to fix it!"

She went to the library and read three books on motor mechanics. She checked out a Chilton's Motor Manual for 1978. Using her dad's tools and things she borrowed from the neighbors, she succeeded in pulling the motor and setting it up in the back yard.

"Ann, look at you," her mother said, "Grease from head to toe, and night after night."

"But, Mom," she said peering from under a grimy cap with strands of blonde hair falling out, "I'm *doing* something, something I really want to do. I think I'm actually going to finish it. The crank system works, and I've almost got the valves back in place."

By Thanksgiving the Camaro was back together again—and running. She gave her Grandma a ride home after the Thanksgiving dinner.

"And listen, grandma, "Doesn't it sound great? Even the tappets are running smooth."

"You sound pretty proud, Sweetie-pie." (Grandma always called her "Sweetie-pie. That was to distinguish her from her sister, "Lambie-pie.")

"Just as good as any boy," said Ann.

"What have boys got to do with it?"

"Well, now I don't have to depend on them. I don't have to stand at the side of the road when my car breaks down and depend on the mercy of some guy to bail me out. I can fix it myself."

"Is that what this is all about? Being better than the men in this world?"

"No, Grandma, It's about me being better than *I've* ever been. Don't you see? If I can do this, I can do anything!"

There's a sequel to this story. The following Christmas, there were six girls in the Camaro. Of course, they were going to a party. The motor was humming beautifully and they were on the eleventh verse of the "Twelve Days of Christmas." Suddenly the wheels hit a patch of ice and headed into the opposite lane. To avoid an oncoming car, Ann steered across the road and into the ditch. The Camaro wrapped itself around a fir tree. One girl broke her arm. The others were just bruised.

Ann smashed her mouth into the steering wheel. Two thousand dollars' worth of orthodontia burst from her mouth in a twisted, bleeding tangle.

"Hma har, Hma har (my car, my car)," was all she could say. All that work for nothing.

"But it wasn't for nothing, after all," she told me. "I proved I could do anything. It changed my thinking. Now I know I can be responsible and accomplish anything with my life. Maybe someday I'll finish those mittens too."

Questions for Reflection

What are you proud of creating or completing?

Have you started something that you still want to complete?

How important is it to prove that you can do something difficult?

Does the passion for achievement help you understand someone near you"?

---

*The sole meaning of
life is to serve
humanity.*

Leo Tolstoy

MAKING A CONTRIBUTION

Close to achievement is contribution. We don't have to climb far up the road to find contribution. It thrives in the same workaday world as achievement.

The difference between achievement and contribution lies not in the action but in the intention. Not *what* is done, but *why*. The meaning of achievement is to succeed at a difficult task ... to do what others can't ... to win ... to get results ... to finish what you have started. In contrast, the meaning of contribution is to do something that *benefits* human civilization. To make a contribution, the task does not have to be difficult. It only has to be useful. You don't have to win; you just have to, well, contribute.

This insight adds zest to the work of many ordinary people. The carpenter doesn't just nail boards together. He builds houses for people to live in. The bank teller doesn't just count money. She keeps money flowing in the economy. Unskilled janitors and garbage collectors contribute to the beauty of the world. As Neil, the maintenance man in our building, once said, "Yup, somebody has to keep 'er lookin' good."

The Law of Contribution

"The purpose of a business," says Larry Wilson, "is not to make money but to help people. Making money is a secondary objective that follows from making a contribution. Doing well (financially) is the reward for doing good."

My friend, David McNally, author of *Even Eagles Need a Push*, is one of the people who encouraged me to write this book. He calls this form of meaning the "law of contribution." He says we all have to work. If we don't work, we don't eat. That's the law of survival. But our souls are dead if that's all we work for. To be alive at work we have to work *for something*. What's important, he says, is to "make a difference."

People Who Make a Difference

Mary is such a contributor. Like Ruth, whom I mentioned earlier, Mary started as a secretary around the same time. Mary is still a secretary, though now to an executive. She works steadily and tirelessly—the truly devoted and loyal worker. She finishes every assignment with high quality. When I asked her once why she worked so hard—this was on a Saturday afternoon when I was pursuing some work demon of my own—she said, "I don't know. I just like to do it. Besides, So-and-So needs it by Monday."

I once thought she worked extra hard for the money. She has a large wardrobe. But after ten years, her dedication is still the same. She does it because it needs to be done. She does it to be useful.

Denny is another contributor. He fixes things—anything mechanical. He is 50'ish and a little on the heavy side. At home he restores old cars in his garage. One of his best is a green '32 Chevy coupe. At work he fixes electrical equipment, like TV cameras, playback machines, and the electro-pneumatic machines we use to wind audio tapes. Somebody once said of him, "If I had to be stuck on a desert island with just one other person, I'd want it to be Denny, because he can make anything work."

But Denny's real contribution is not his mechanical talent. Neither is it a spirit of working for humankind. "I don't do just anything, ya know," he told me once. So he has his pride and his limits.

The something extra he brings is worry. He worries whether all the repairs are going to be finished on time. He worries about how long before a machine will break down again. He worries about keeping everyone happy. I don't want him to worry, but it's comforting to know that he does. It means that he cares. It means that he finds more significance in the job than his apprentice who sits woodenly at the workbench from eight to five and solders things.

Promoting a Deeper Value

Some people take the philosophy of contribution even further. They believe that their work promotes some deeper value. A treatment center in our town helps chemically dependent teen-agers. This is a noble cause in itself—to contribute to the health of young human beings. That's why I joined their Board of Directors. But there is something extra in the air at this place. When speaking to referral agents and other professionals, the employees talk about "being in the treatment business ... helping kids and families function better ... making them into useful members of society ... etc." Straight-forward, professional language. But in their hearts most of the employees believe that they are in the "love" business—helping kids to love themselves, their families, and the world. It's an added dimension in the work. It adds a level of dedication that makes the treatment itself better—and the work more meaningful.

Rose is the cook at this center. She has serious excema on her arms which she covers with the white sleeves of her uniform. Every day she cooks two hot meals for fifty youth and two dozen staff members. After setting out the food, she comes into the dining room and sits at one of the tables. There are only ten tables, so eventually some teens sit down with her.

"So, how bad was the treatment today, kiddo?" she asks.

"Nothin' special," someone says.

"Then how come you're so hungry?" she teases.

"I'm always hungry."

"Good, then I'll always have a job."

Later when the kids go back to their classes and just the staff on lunch break are sitting around, Rose unwraps a piece of candy and says, "I'm like their mother, you know. Those kids need a mother."

The Trojan Horse

In my own business we call this idea of promoting a deeper value the "Trojan Horse." I work for a management consulting and training firm. We believe that we make a double contribution. What customers buy from us are techniques for improving productivity and performance. That's the outside of the horse. They wouldn't spend much money for what's inside the horse—namely ideas that help the workers to find more *fulfillment* in their work. But that's what we really have in mind.

Eldon was a tough union steward I once had in class. "I'm on to you," he said. "You're not teaching us customer relations skills at all. Without saying so, you're teaching us to love these people, just like they tell us in church."

"Does that make you feel better about the job?" I asked.

"Yeah," he said after a moment, "I guess it does."

Working for Nothing

I haven't always been so successful in promoting the value of contribution. One night I was low on gas so I pulled into a filling station that closes at 11:00 PM. It was 10:55. After putting the nozzle in the filler tube, I looked for a squeegee to wash the windshield. I couldn't find one in any of the buckets on the pump island, so I went inside to ask.

There were two people on duty, a woman cashier and a stocky young attendant. "Where's the washer stick?" I asked.

"Over there," the stocky young man said. "Bring it in when you come back, would you. We're almost closed up." I found the tool amid the air hoses and display frames that had been piled up for the night between the merchandise shelves.

I washed the windows and put the gas hose back. Just then another car pulled in. It was now two minutes to eleven. The other driver asked for the squeegee to wash his own windows. I gave it to him and told him about bringing it in.

As the cashier ran off my credit card, the young attendant opened a fuse box on the wall and turned off the driveway lights. "Hey," shouted the cashier, "you left that guy out there in the dark."

"I know," he replied. He seemed to be addressing me as much as her. "But if I leave the lights on, someone else will drive in at just the last minute. And then we'll have to work for nothing."

"Work for nothing?" I said astonished. "I can't even count the times I worked for nothing."

"Well, that's too bad," he said. "But at eleven bells I'm out of here." Apparently for this young man work is only a necessary evil, measured in time and not in contribution. Its significance is in what it pays for—and the time it takes away from other things.

I passed the other driver at the door, as he entered from the darkened driveway. I noted with satisfaction that he had the wash stick in his hand. I got in my car.

Maybe that fellow has a passion for some other form of meaning, I thought to myself. But as I drove away I saw only the last few lights go out.

Making History

Some people see their contribution as part of a much larger destiny. They see themselves as agents in the great work of history. Karl Marx and his mentor, G.W.F. Hegel, were the first to raise our consciousness about *actively and consciously cooperating* with the march of history. How exciting and meaningful to join others in bringing about a world that is inspired and even assured by the laws of history!

Certainly the Kennedy brothers, John and Robert, saw themselves as leaders in this kind of work. "Ask not what your country can do for you, but what you can do for your country," are words we all remember. And Robert Kennedy said, "Few have the greatness to bend the events of history. But each person can affect a certain parcel of events. So, with numberless courageous acts we build the future."

Jane is a person who takes these words seriously. By appearance she is an unlikely agent of history—quiet and unassuming. She married a doctor and lives in a comfortable house near Minnehaha Creek. She never read Hegel or Marx or the philosophers of progressive history, but in the 60's her heroes were John Kennedy and Hubert Humphrey. She worked on their political campaigns—no speeches, but she passed out literature and asked friends what *they* were going to do for their country.

Today, in her 60's, she still supports candidates who promote her vision of history. She astonishes other doctors' wives with questions about how they plan to improve human rights in Guatemala. Her favorite technique is to invite friends to what seems like a "social" event. Sometimes it *is* just a social event, but other times she surprises you with a challenging question or a controversial guest. One time she opened a big box of coffee from Nicaragua and asked us all to buy some. This was at a time when the United States government was, wrongly in her view, opposing the government of Nicaragua.

For Jane it's inevitable that the laws of history will eventually bring about greater justice in the world. Her role is to collaborate consciously with it—however gently, however indirectly. Yes, I bought the coffee. How could I not help her with such a noble task?

Building the Kingdom of God

Actually, the philosophy of contribution has long inspired emissaries from the world's great religions. It is implied, for example, in the zeal of Christian apostles to spread the "kingdom of God" in the world. Some, like the American pilgrims, crossed the Atlantic to create colonies of the kingdom. Others, like Isaac Jogues, gave up everything to live and work with primitive people. And some like my cousin, Gretchen, do it from home.

A Modern Missionary

Gretchen is a career woman. She felt lucky that her relationship with Dick, a successful advertising printer, started her in business at an early age. After Dick's unexpected death, she was even better off. While she didn't really inherit the business, she did inherit the clients because they liked her. In a way, she had it all. And yet she didn't. She missed Dick. And she missed a deeper sense of meaning.

A picture in Time Magazine caught her eye. It showed a forlorn Peruvian girl living in poverty. "Save the Children," said the caption. There was an address in a box under the picture. Yes, she responded on the form, she would like to "sponsor" a child. Maybe this would bring the meaning she was looking for.

The papers arrived in ten days. She could sponsor Maria. Over the years Gretchen contributed a good sum of money for Maria's care and education. A big part of her reward was the letters, 34 of them, with ever-steady progress in length, English and interest. Eventually, she arranged for Maria to study in the United States, and for her to live with Gretchen and Don. (She had now married her second business partner).

For a while Gretchen believed that she would be a kind of "mother" to Maria. This fit because she didn't have any children of her own. She adopted Maria, but the adoption did not last. The girl who moved into her home was not the girl she had sponsored. Maria was bright enough for letters and studies, but she was not socially communicative. Besides she stole things. Not just a few things but many. And not just from Gretchen, but from everyone. After many tears Gretchen accepted that Maria was an incurable kleptomaniac and gave up trying to change her.

I don't know what became of Maria, except that she stopped living with Gretchen. But Gretchen found new children to sponsor. She continues to give money and hospitality. Her house is always full of foreign students and their friends.

"I decided I'm not cut out to be a mother, like my sister-in-law," she said. "I like being a sponsor. It's sort of like being a missionary." That's not exactly what Hegel or Marx or Isaac Jogues had in mind, but it is conscious cooperation with the progress of history.

What "Shallow" Dave Discovered

Remember my friends Susan, Grace and Dave? Over the course of many conversations, each discovered a special source of meaning. What Dave discovered was that he was only "shallow" where others *expected* him to find meaning. Actually, he felt deeply about making a contribution, but never had the words for it. In the end he told it like this:

"What I do for a living is deliver packages. At first I was a driver, then I got into management. Like Barb says, I like being a manager. If you asked me a few years ago about what I do, I wouldn't have called it making a contribution. I just saw it as making a living. We deliver packages all over the country—all over the world, actually. And we pride ourselves on fast, efficient service. Then I began to look at it another way. What was I feeling good about when I did it? I started thinking about what was actually in the packages—you know, papers and small machine parts, but also flowers, blueprints, books, chemicals, and pets. We even shipped a human heart once for a transplant. So I got to thinking that what we ship are things that people need for their lives and their businesses. I mean, the contribution isn't just in the shipping; it's in getting useful stuff to people.

"For example, this one Friday we were supposed to deliver a wedding dress. The package was delayed coming in, so it didn't go on the regular delivery truck. All the drivers had already gone home for the day and only a few of us office-types were left at the depot. The wedding was Saturday, and the bride's mother had been calling frantically all day. In fact, she was downright abusive, and some of the guys wanted to make her come down and pick it up from the night clerk. Anyway, I drove it to her house on my way home. I sure didn't do it out of love for the girl's mother. I guess I did it because I just couldn't picture a wedding without a happy bride. So wasn't that making a contribution?"

We all agreed that Dave had a lot more depth than he usually gave himself credit for.

Questions for Reflection

Who benefits from your work? What good does it do for society?

In what ways do you make a difference—however large, however small?

How are you contributing to the large forces sweeping human history?

Who is like Dave in your life—yourself, or someone close to you?

---

*Adventure, pal, is
what makes you feel
alive, really alive.*

Papillon

GOING ON A GREAT ADVENTURE

Emerging from the business district with all its serious dedication to achievement and contribution, we realize we are only part way through the Realm of Doing. Up ahead the road zigzags wildly into the mountains. It bids us to leave all this sober and civilized action behind and do something crazy. So, let's go on an adventure. Who says, after all, that meaning can't be fun?

Facing Down a Glacier

The kids were about three paces ahead when it happened. We were tramping through large boulders at the bottom of an Alpine gorge, trying to get a closer look at the glacier. They were cute kids about seven and nine. Their mother, Lynne, sent them with me, so she could chat with Dorothy on a picnic blanket. The three of us had cooked up this holiday in Switzerland to get away from our studies in neighboring Germany. Both their husbands had stayed behind to prepare for exams without the usual family din.

The glacier loomed high before me and the kids—a huge wall of dirty ice topped with white snow. We picked our way between the large boulders at its foot. Suddenly a sharp crack echoed through the gorge. I knew that glaciers melted, but I never guessed that the sun caused them to explode. Glancing up, I saw rocks and snow rolling down the wall right over us.

Too late I realized why the Swiss had built an elaborate viewing stand on the other side of the gorge—out of range from the falling ice and rock. It was also a quick lesson in geology: glaciers are not all ice. The huge boulders we were walking among had once been *part* of the glacier.

I lunged at the kids who were just starting to look around at the loud noise. I grabbed their shoulders and pulled them down under my chest. We rolled in a heap—one soft boulder among several hard ones. As I waited for the falling rocks to hit us, one thought screamed in my ears. "It's been a hell of an adventure!" Thud, thud, thud. "And they're not even my kids!" Thud, thud.

When the noise stopped I looked up. The warm sun still glistened off the glacier. Just like two moments before. It was as if nothing had happened. Just a few more stones in the valley. It would have looked the same had we been killed. In the distance Lynne and Dorothy were still chatting. They hadn't even noticed.

The kids were crying, not from the danger, but because I had knocked their heads together trying to save them. Some hero. I even had to argue with them to move off to safety. But it was a hell of an adventure.

Adventure adds a lot of meaning to life. The high emotional state—the feeling of being outside of yourself, of taking a risk, and doing more than you could do with ordinary skill and planning. The feeling that the gods are carrying you.

One Great Adventure

Some people define their life by a *single* great adventure. One of these is the grandfather in John Steinbeck's *Red Pony*.

One day a letter arrived at the Tiflin farm announcing that Grandfather would be coming that same day. The boy, Jody, was excited. It meant that Grandfather would tell stories about crossing the plains when he was the leader of a wagon train. But it was not exciting news to Jody's father, Carl. "I've heard that story about a thousand times," he complained. "He just goes on and on, and he never changes a word in the things he tells." To ease the situation Jody's mother tried to explain:

"Look at it this way, Carl. That was the big thing in my father's life. He led a wagon train clear across the plains to the coast, and when it was finished, his life was done. It was a big thing to do, but it didn't last long enough. Look," she continued, "it's as though he was born to do that, and after he finished it, there wasn't anything more for him to do but think about it and talk about it. If there'd been any farther west to go, he'd have gone."

Carl promised to be patient and pretend to listen. But when Grandfather arrived he started his old singsong narrative and made such a bore of himself that Carl broke his promise. Grandfather overheard Carl complain: "It's finished. Nobody wants to hear about it over and over."

Later the old man told Jody that he would probably be leaving soon because of how people felt. He admitted, "I tell those stories, but they're not what I want to tell. I only know how I want people to feel when I tell them." He said that "westering" was the great adventure that everyone deeply felt at the time.

"We all carried life out here and set it down the way those ants carry eggs. And I was the leader. The westering was as big as God, and the slow steps that made the movement piled up and piled up until the continent was crossed.

"Then we came down to the sea, and it was done." He stopped and wiped his eyes until the rims were red. ... "Your father is right. It is finished."

John Steinbeck, Red Pony, NY, Bantam, 1937, pp. 78 and 89ff.

That's the way it is with some of us. We live an adventure so great that its meaning consumes our lives—even when it's over.

I'm Coming to Get You, You Crazy Bastard

Other people live a hundred adventures. For example, my father-in-law, John, was a fast-driving, hard-drinking, Irish Chicago cop. Every moment of his life reads like an episode from Hill Street Blues.

One time he and a new partner pulled up to a favorite watering hole after their watch. Without warning they were startled into action. Carrigan, the owner, lay dead behind the bar. Shot in the head. His wife was screaming that Hurlehy, the hired man, had gone off his rocker and pulled a gun in an argument.

"It wasn't about anything," she sobbed. "And then he ran down the basement."

"Where is he now?" John asked.

"Still down there."

John cracked open the door and shouted, "Hey, Hurlehy, come up here." Only a toneless laughter came back from the darkness below. "Okay, you crazy bastard, I'm coming to get you."

He slipped quickly into the stairway without presenting a silhouette. He bounced down the stairs low on his buttocks.

"Where are you?" he growled. This time a bullet came back in reply. For a minute they exchanged gunfire in the dark. Then holding his flashlight at arms-length to one side, he finally caught sight of Hurlehy behind a pillar. He clicked off the light and slowly inched forward. Then he made his favorite kind of arrest, punching Hurlehy once in the stomach to knock the wind out of him.

Upstairs, he told his rookie partner to take the handcuffed prisoner out to the car. By this time other cops were starting to arrive. John stood with them at the bar, triumphant, and downed a few drinks. He got involved with calling the coroner and calming down the hysterical wife.

Twenty minutes later he saw his partner alone in the back hall. "What the hell are you doing here?" he asked. "Where's Hurlehy?"

"Well," said the rookie, "the two on-duty guys said they'd take him into the station."

"The hell they will," said John. "He's our collar and I'm not going to let those bastards take the credit." So he ran out the back door just in time to step in front of the departing squad car.

"Let him out!" he shouted. The cops inside shook their heads "no." So John drew his pistol and pointed it through the driver's window. "Let him out," he repeated.

Two days later he was called downtown to the chief's office. "What's this I hear about you threatening two officers with a gun?" growled the chief.

"They were out of line. They had no right to grab my collar."

"You were out of line," shot back the chief. "Listen, Hughes," he said sitting down, "you're a hell of a cop. But you're too damned hot headed. You act without thinking. I suppose that's your good point as well as your bad."

"Yes, sir," said John, "I was just reacting to what was happening. I can see in hindsight that I let it go too far." John was better at asking for forgiveness than for permission.

"Get out of here," said the chief. "But for chrissake control your temper. And if this ever happens again, you're through."

"Yes, sir."

And so he lived from one exciting adventure to the next. Unlike Jody's grandfather he never stopped. He only slowed down enough to appease the brass.

A Youthful Journey to the East

An adventure early in life can give meaning to the rest of one's days. Often this defining youthful adventure is a journey. Such journeys are the stuff of legends: St. George off to slay dragons, Lancelot to find the Holy Grail, and Beauty to charm the beast. Adventures of this sort, says Joseph Campbell, awaken a new character in the youth and set a pattern for meaning all through life. Here is such a "legend" told me by a young man named Oscar. Here's his story in his own words.

It started, he said, by painting curbs in small towns in Ohio. It wasn't very noble work, but we made a lot of money. Me and Duane, we'd drive to some "virgin" town, one without painted numbers, and we'd get permission from the town administrator. Then we'd go up and down the streets stenciling house numbers on the curbs. There'd always be plenty of kids to put our leaflets in the mailboxes.

This is what they said:

D and O Number Systems

- Uniform addressing system
- Easy to find in the dark
- Adds to your security

With the permission and encouragement of city management.

The best towns were the ones with pools. We'd paint in the morning and swim in the afternoon. Then in the evening we'd come back to collect for our services. Surprisingly, just about everybody gave us something. Some people, though, got upset, said we were cheats, and told us to get out. Cost of doing business, I guess.

At the pool in the afternoon we dreamed about what we *really* wanted to do—bicycle across the country, "from sea to shining sea." We talked about how we would sleep under the stars and make it all the way on our own. We talked ourselves into it and decided to do it the next summer.

We chose to go from West to East because, according to the weatherman, the prevailing wind would be on our backs. That's important on a bicycle. My parents arranged their vacation so they could drive us to Astoria, Oregon, right on the Pacific Ocean. I have a blown-up picture in my room of me and Duane with our wheels in the water.

It didn't start very well, though. I felt a lump in my throat as my parents drove off. Here we were alone and a little scared. Then it started to rain, and even though it was June, it was quite cold.

But we got on with it. We each carried 35 pounds of gear in two baskets, called panniers, mounted over the back wheels.

Going over the mountains we carried the extra weight of our parkas, which we later mailed home. One time we stopped at the top of a pass to check our equipment.

"How are you doin', Duane?"

"Freezing my ass. I'm worried about my knees giving out. If it was cold coming up, it's going to be ten times worse going down."

"You know what I'm dreaming about, Duane?"

"A warm fire."

"Yeah, and a cup of hot cocoa."

"Well, you aren't going to find it in this godforsaken place. So let's shove off and hope for the best."

Just around the second bend, we rolled onto a fabulous sun-lit vista. Off to the left we saw a cabin with smoke coming from the chimney. When we got closer it turned out to be a tavern. Inside there was a beautiful wooden bar. The proprietor told us it had been hauled up by wagons from Boston in the late eighteen hundreds.

"Why don't you boys sit by the fire while I fix you something from the bar. Just name your poison."

"Cocoa," I said.

"Yeah," chimed in Duane, "hot cocoa."

Some days later we came out of the mountains in Wyoming. Our goal was seventy to ninety miles a day. We were traveling back roads and there weren't many towns on our route. Coasting downhill we made eighty-five miles in the morning, and the next town after this one was another eighty miles out in the plains. We sat in the Dairy Queen and pored over the map. Should we stay in this town with its nice campground or go for the next town? We finally decided to go for it and pick up an extra day.

What we didn't know is how different the plains are from the mountains. We wore parkas in the morning. We never expected by mid-afternoon to be sweating like pigs and dodging rattle snakes on the sun-baked asphalt. Around three I got a flat tire. I waved Duane on and stopped to fix it. It was on the rear tire so I had to remove the panniers and take the whole thing apart. I used some of my little remaining water to find the leak. It took about an hour. When I remounted I could tell I had lost a lot of strength. Two hours later I caught up with Duane. He had stopped to wait in the shade of an old mining shack. You never go back unless it's absolutely necessary. So he had just waited.

We were both out of water and worried because we had stopped sweating. There was nothing to do but push on. We flagged down two campers, but neither had any water to give us. All I could do was dream about an oasis and keep the pedals turning. If we stopped it might be the end.

By nightfall we hit a few shanties. Then a few more. It didn't seem like much of a town, just some sheds and houses scattered around. But there must have been quite a few people because they told us to stay at the new high school down the road.

Do you know what they had at the school? A swimming pool! Gallons and gallons of cool water. Later, after a few beers around the pool, I said, "What do you think, Duane, should we go out and paint some curbs for these good people?"

"It sure is a 'virgin' town," he said. "They don't even have roads much less a uniform numbering system."

We covered 3,750 miles that summer. It took three months to do it. By the time we made Iowa, we were old pro's. We could handle anything. The only challenge was the sheer duration of it. We thought about stopping home in Ohio. But that would be like giving up. We joked a lot about finding a good excuse to quit:

"What if we got hit by a Winnebago?"

"I'd rather just fall and break a leg."

"Yeah, but we wouldn't get in the papers that way."

Finally, we pulled into Norfolk, Virginia and rolled straight for the beach. I've got a second blown-up photograph on my wall, this time with our wheels in the Atlantic Ocean.

The Beginning, the Middle and the End

Two things have stayed with me from this adventure, Oscar continued to tell me. One is that something will always turn up when I need it—a cup of cocoa or an oasis in the desert. Whenever things are going badly, I think back on the trip and draw power from it.

The other thing is that life itself is like an adventure. It has a beginning, a middle and an end. When we first started out we were like little kids, cold and scared, not knowing if the map was accurate and maybe we would have to call our parents if we got lost. Then there was a kind of reckless adolescence when we took stupid chances and didn't bring enough water. Then there was a long maturity, filled with confidence and dogged determination. Finally, there was the end when we raced for the finish and stood there like fools in the Atlantic— joyful that we had made it and sad that it was over.

I guess, he concluded, I would sum up life's adventure by saying: it has an exciting beginning, an arduous middle and a bitter-sweet end.

Questions for Reflection

What is the most exciting thing you have done in your life? Is it over or still going on?

How much uncertainty, inconvenience and danger can you tolerate? Or do you revel in it?

What lessons did you draw from the most difficult adventure you ever had?

*We must do what
the gods did in the
beginning.*

Satapatha Brahmana

FOLLOWING HONORED TRADITIONS

Emerging from so much adventure, our thoughts may be diverging in a thousand ways. So let's regroup here at this ancient campsite. The fire circle draws us back together again. The camp sits in a clearing just below the tree line where the steep path through the Realm of Doing passes into the mountains. You can tell that many generations have rested here before. The ground is trodden, the stones worn, and a sign says that many flint tools have been discovered in the area.

These primeval surroundings make us wonder about the *direction* of the activity we have been observing in the Realm of Doing. Most of what we have seen—achieving, contributing, adventuring—is aimed at the future. Always moving forward; always something new. But novelty is not an essential attribute of meaning. In fact, many people find meaning in the opposite direction—in repeating what others have done in the past.

Doing What We Are Expected to Do

The best spokesman for this sense of meaning is the affable, dairyman, Tevye, from *Fiddler on the Roof.* He sings about tradition:

Because of our traditions, we've kept our balance for many, many years. Here in Anatevka we have traditions for everything—how to eat, how to sleep, how to wear clothes. For instance, we always keep our heads covered and always wear a little prayer shawl. This shows our constant devotion to God. You may ask, how did this tradition start? I'll tell you—I don't know. But it's a tradition. Because of our traditions, everyone knows who he is and what God expects him to do.

Well, you probably know the story: the clearly defined roles of the papa, the mama, the daughters, the matchmaker and the rabbi—and the terrible consternation they suffer when the customs are broken.

The value of traditions is that meaning is built into them. They are ready-made formulas that spare us from having to constantly invent new meaning. It may be hard sometimes to do what the traditions require, but for many people there is great satisfaction in knowing that one has been faithful to these proven patterns.

Living in the Golden Age

The meaning of tradition is strongest in primitive societies who live close to the cycles of nature. People of these cultures feel keenly the succession of the seasons, the rounds of the sun, the return of the moon, the ebb and flow of the waters, the periods of fertility and the passing of the generations.

Ancient people celebrate these repetitions as sacred events. They tell stories (or "myths") about how the gods set the pattern in the Golden Age of creation. They dance and act out the stories as if reenacting what the gods and heroes did in that special time. The experience can be so powerful that, as Mircea Eliade says, "the man of a traditional culture:

> sees himself as real [that is, having meaning] only to the extent that he ceases to be himself and is satisfied with imitating and repeating the gestures of another."
>
> *Mircea Eliade, Cosmos and History,*
> *NY Harper and Row, 1959, p. 34.*

I once caught a glimpse of this meaning when I visited some Indian ruins in Arizona. The Sinagua inhabited the Verde Valley from about the 12th to the 15th centuries. Archeologists had dug up their tools, cooking utensils, farm implements, cloth fragments, religious symbols, even their toys. The Sinagua were basically farmers. They cultivated the fields next to the river. What a sensible place, I thought, to try farming (as if I was surprised that primitive people could be so smart).

The Sinagua were also builders. At the same time my forefathers were erecting castles and cathedrals in Europe, these people were building stone dwellings hundreds of feet up in the bluffs over a river in America. I could almost hear their voices—making plans about where to put the next wall, debating whose turn it was to bury the garbage, and warning the kids not to get too close to the edge of the cliff. I felt one with those people. We were bound by history and tradition. When I tell my children it's their turn to take out the garbage, I know that even this simple act is filled with meaning because it has been consecrated by millennia of human repetition. There is something eternal about what we do over and over.

I get a similar feeling when I see new parents doing with their children what I did with mine, or what my parents did with me. How we love to repeat what the gods and heroes have done before us, even when we think we are making it up for the first time.

Golf is Not a Tradition

In modern society we are less likely to view our deeds as repetitions of mythic events or natural cycles. But we are not so removed from the cycles of nature to miss celebrating them altogether. Most of our public holidays like Thanksgiving,

New Year and Passover follow the seasons. And, of course, we mark the completion of our personal cycles with a birthday.

Aunt Julia makes more of this than anybody. She lives by the calendar. She likes the kind you get at a religious goods store, with red markings for holidays and feast days. When she buys a new calendar she copies in the birthdays and anniversaries of all her family members and friends. That way she won't forget to send the right card from the abundant supply in the left-hand drawer of her mahogany secretary.

The most important days she colors with yellow highlighter. These are the glorious days of celebration— like Thanksgiving, Christmas and Mother's Day. They are to be observed in a certain way: church in the morning, visiting relatives in the afternoon, and a big meal in the evening. Certain events require an exchange of gifts; others, a display of flowers; and others, a special ritual, like watching the Rose Bowl parade, shooting off firecrackers, or looking at the family album.

I remember one Mother's Day when we teenagers, including her son, did not follow the script. "How could you do this!" she complained angrily when we arrived in the late afternoon.

"We're here," we said, "and we went to church this morning too."

"I don't care," she admonished, "you just don't go off to play golf on Mother's Day!"

And so we learned the hard way the traditions of our heritage.

Reliving the Deeds of the Lord

We moderns are most involved with repetition in the practice of religion. Here we bathe ourselves in tradition. We listen to messages from the past as guides to action. The example of the Saints demands imitation, both in life and liturgy. I discovered the power of this meaning one afternoon on a family trip through the southeastern United States.

"Boyd," I said into the mouthpiece of a roadside phone. "B-o-y-d, Boyd on Old Mill Road."

"No number for Boyd, sir," came back the operator. "Maybe they don't have a phone."

"Everyone has a phone," I said somewhat testily.

"Not back in those hills, sir. People can be very different back thar."

So it was with some uncertainty that I headed the family wagon up the Smokey Mountains near Ashville to visit our old neighbors. They had moved here three years before in search of a new space, closer to Nature and God. We had been touring in a wide loop around the Southeast and hoped to visit them on our way home. Failing the phone call, we were forced to rely on the sketchy directions they had sent by letter.

The directions proved accurate. We found Old Mill Road. And exactly a mile and a half past the stone bridge was the dirt road leading up to their house. It was a mobile home perched on a cement protrusion with a commanding view of the valley below and the mountains across. It had electricity feeding a new refrigerator, a water heater, and a stove—but no telephone.

Our friends, Cherry and Don, were even expecting us, plus or minus a day, based on our own letter. After we settled in and the kids ran off to climb in the hills, Don said, "I have an errand to run before supper. Do you want to come with me?"

"Sure," I said. He picked up a heavy lunch basket and we drove off in his truck.

"This is an errand of mercy," he explained. "There's an old couple in our church, named Seth and Mary. He's one of the elders, and she is dying of cancer. We're all taking turns bringing a daily meal. We've got a hot dish for tonight and some sandwiches for tomorrow."

"I take it then, you're pretty well settled in a church here?"

"Oh, yes," he said. "This is a very religious place and we feel quite at home." As we drove the twenty miles toward the small town where Seth and Mary lived, I wondered what sort of Bible Belt community this might be.

The old couple lived in a brown bungalow at the edge of town. The yard was well trimmed and abundant with colorful flower beds. Seth unlatched the screen door and greeted us in a strong voice. After thanking us for the food he said, "Mary's asleep and we don't have to worry about waking her up. The hospice nurse gave her something about an hour ago. So why don't you boys just sit a spell." We agreed. It seemed like a nice thing to do, to visit the infirm and the aged. Seth got some Cokes out of the refrigerator.

"I'm sorry about your wife," I said. "It must be very hard for you."

"Yes, it's hard," he replied wistfully, "but it gives me a chance to think about the meaning of it all. It's the way of the Cross."

"You mean that it's God's will?" I asked, reaching for what I thought might be his fundamentalist theology.

"I suppose you could say that," he rejoined. "But I think of it more as another step in following the way of Jesus. You see what I believe is that we are graced by re-living the life of the Lord. "

"I see," I said somewhat surprised.

"Times like this," he continued, "when I'm losing what I really love, I can only bear it because it's like when God gave his only son so that others could have life. Or like Jesus himself who said, 'Into thy hands I commend my spirit.' We're all part of a great mystery which he lived before us."

"So the idea is that life gets its meaning from doing what Jesus did," I said, trying to interpret. I was beginning to realize that the man had a deeper theology than I had suspected.

"The idea is," he clarified, "that God is leading us somewhere. Like he led the chosen people out of bondage and into the promised-land. He's leading me and Mary somewhere too—out of our comfortable but somehow narrow life to some better promised land. The fact that he did these things himself once gives me the courage to let it happen to me too."

"You seem to be a man of great faith," I said.

Don leaned into the conversation and said, "I think we all have this faith to some degree. That's why 'remembering' is an important part of what we do at church. We listen to the readings to remember the great acts of the Lord, and we break bread to remember the Last Supper. He told us to do this to remember him."

"Mary loved those services," mused Seth. "That kind of remembering made it all worthwhile for her. Every day of her grown up life she devoted to cooking and cleaning and doing a lot of little things. Whenever we sat down to the evening meal she didn't want us to just say grace. She wanted us to remember the Last Supper. This helped her remember that the little things we do are really great things. We do what Jesus did. Even now in dying she is doing what God himself has done."

Later that evening back on the mountain we sat on the porch and watched the sun go down behind a large peak. It made deep shadows in the valley. Cherry served some wine she had made in an old cider jug. She called it "modern moonshine." When we sat down to eat Don looked at me as he said grace. "We remember Seth and Mary in our prayers," he said. "And we especially thank God for this meal. We recall how Jesus ate with his friends on the night before he died."

All the voices around me gave the ritual response: "Amen."

"Amen," I repeated, "Amen."

Questions for Reflection

What traditions do you celebrate in your family? Where did these practices come from?

What do you do over and over that millions of others have done before you?

Who are your heroes? How do you follow in their footsteps?

Who in your family cares the most about your traditions?

*Nothing can possibly be
conceived in the world
or even out of it, which
can be called good,
without qualification,
except a good will.*

Emmanuel Kant

DOING THE RIGHT THING

Our last stop in the Realm of Doing is a town at the end of the road. The town center is unsurprisingly like every other in the world. Behind its proud avenues, respectable store fronts and public monuments is a tangle of back alleys, cheap hotels and seedy pleasure parlors. Its very composition symbolizes a struggle that defines the meaning of life for many people. It's the struggle between virtue and vice.

We all engage in the struggle to some degree. That's because virtue is acquired and not inherited. It is a choice, and it is not easy. Neither is it always clear what is the right thing to do.

Yet some people find more meaning in the struggle than others. They see life as a series of efforts to do the right thing. For them, virtue, honor and integrity occupy the center stage and turn life into a great moral drama.

The meaning of action for these fellow travelers is not in "making" something or "experiencing" something—as with others in the Realm of Doing—but in performing actions that measure up to certain standards. It's not doing the useful thing, the exciting thing or the traditional thing that produces the meaning. It's doing the *right* thing.

The key to meaning here lies in deciding which standards are "right" and then having the courage to live up to them.

Men of Honor

One summer when my brother and I were still trying to choose our paths in life, we traveled with our parents to the Arrowhead country in northern Minnesota. We drove to a picturesque resort on Big Bear Lake just outside the Boundary Waters Canoe Area. The resort was operated by two men, Darryl and Bob, who advertised it as clean, cultured and rustic.

On the drive up we passed through Grand Marais, the county seat of Cook County, where the Gunflint Trail turns north away from Lake Superior. My second brother, Phil, who is ten years younger, was with us. As we approached the sandstone courthouse on the right he said, "Is that the place where you spent the night in jail?"

"Yes," I admitted reluctantly, even though I had been thinking about it for the last twenty miles.

"Let's stop and look at it," he said excitedly.

"Nah, I don't want to."

"Yeah," piped in my brother Jim. "Show us where you went astray."

I was about to protest when Dad pulled into a filling station. "We need gas," he said. "There might not be any stations up the Trail. You can all do what you want for ten minutes." The car stopped and I knew I was trapped.

"C'mon, Tom," said Mother, "just for the fun of it." Some fun. This was the place that called me a criminal, and my own family treated it like a tourist attraction.

Crossing the street I pictured that evening three years before when five of us teenagers drove up to Cook County to hunt bears. We had been told by a DNR ranger at the State Fair that you could shoot bears anywhere in the state. He forgot to mention: *anywhere but* Cook County. When we asked a local garage attendant where we could find some bears, he told us about a refuse dump a mile out of Grand Marais.

We reached the dump at twilight and unpacked our rifles. There was just enough light to hunt by. About five black bears were digging for garbage fifty feet below at the bottom of the landfill. A dozen other people were also at the rim—some locals dumping trash, and some tourists watching the bears.

My friends were all excited. "Wow, this is our chance," they were saying as they fumbled with their stocks, bolts and barrels. I started to feel some reluctance as I assembled my shotgun and slowly pushed three slugs into the magazine.

"I don't know if I want to do this," I mumbled, looking down at the bears just standing there pawing through the garbage.

"C'mon," said George. "This is our chance. It's what we came for." He paused. "But if you're chicken..."

"No, I'm not chicken." I cocked the bolt and switched off the safety. A volley of shots rang out. Bang, bang, bang! The other guys were already shooting. The bears wheeled and started to run. I pointed the muzzle downhill and aimed at a retreating figure. Boom! I had never fired a slug before. The gun kicked more than it ever did with buckshot. I don't know if it affected my aim or not. The bear kept moving toward the woods and disappeared in the dusk.

"I think we got one!" someone shouted. Three of my companions ran down the hill to have a look. I stayed at the rim, not too sure about what we had done. I unloaded and waited. A crowd of onlookers started to form on the other side of our car. They didn't look like they approved of our manly deed.

Just then a squad car rolled out of the darkening woods and pulled up behind us. "What's going on here?" asked the officer.

"We're hunting bear," said George still excited and proud.

"Poachers!" shouted someone from the crowd, evidently feeling that it was now safe to express this opinion.

"No," said George, addressing the officer, "you can shoot bear anywhere in the state. A ranger told us so."

"Not in Cook County," replied the policeman. "It's against the law here. Especially in a garbage dump. Did you hit anything?"

"We got one!" shouted one of the scouts climbing back over the rim to give his report. "Ohh," he said weakly, seeing the officer.

"Just like shooting fish in a barrel!" cried out another emboldened voice from the crowd.

"I'm afraid you boys will have to come with me," said the officer. He made us put all the guns in his trunk. Two of us had to ride in the squad car. The rest he ordered to follow in our car to the courthouse in Grand Marais.

We didn't actually spend the night in jail, as my brother imagined. We waited for an hour in the corridor just in front of the cells while the officer summoned a justice of the peace. Then we were led into the judge's office. It was a small room with a big desk. Most of us had to stand. We protested our innocence again, telling about the DNR ranger at the State Fair booth. "Maybe I could let you off," said the judge, "if you were caught out in the woods. But you were apprehended in the public dump with many witnesses. I'm afraid you're going to have to pay for your impetuosity."

He called all of our parents, confiscated our guns and fined us each a hundred dollars.

To ease our ignominy we sent our oldest member into a liquor store to buy a bottle of sloe gin. It was raining and we didn't have any money left for a motel. So we took refuge in the basement of a house under construction and drank away our shame.

"So this is where they locked you up," pronounced Phil passing in front of the three cells in the courthouse.

"They didn't lock us up," I protested again. "They just took away our guns and money."

"Well, well, well," he said, stroking the dull steel bars and gazing into the now-empty cells.

"I think we've seen enough," said Mother mercifully. "Let's drive on to the resort."

When we arrived we found that Darryl and Bob were indeed cultured hosts. They had carved a manicured garden out of the primitive forest. Varnished log cabins nestled in small clearings. All were connected by paths to a grassy expanse on which stood the main, white-painted lodge. Flowers bloomed in pine box beds in all corners of the grounds. Down from the lodge a gleaming metal dock jutted out into the clear water. Next to the dock was a rack of light green canoes stacked three high, their noses neatly aligned like dolphins in a water show. Inside, the lodge walls were covered with new books and tasteful paintings. We liked the mixture of ruggedness and elegance.

One night after supper, Dad, my youngest brother and I came back from a sauna. We could hear voices rising as we entered the family cabin. "But I don't want to be a lawyer," we heard Jim say.

"Lawyers make a lot of money," Mother replied.

"I don't care," insisted Jim. What I do care about is helping people. I think I want to be a social worker."

"Nobody we know is a social worker," she came back. "It's not a real profession. It puts you in the same category as census-takers and baby-sitters."

"Jeez," he said. "Is that all you know about it?"

"What's the big deal?" I ventured, taking my brother's side. "You can make anything you want to out of a job. You can be a lousy lawyer as easily as a great social worker."

Mom started to cry. "I just want you boys to be happy. I hate to see you throwing away your lives on careers you will regret later."

"Can't a person be happy doing what he wants?" suggested Phil somewhat timidly.

Jim laughed. "You wanted to be a garbage-man when you were little. Would that make you happy?"

"Hey, I'm on your side," Phil retorted, starting to feel the bite of this long-standing family argument. "I don't know what I want to do yet. I won't even start college for a couple of years. But I'm going to do something I want."

"You'd probably make a great engineer," said Mom.

"There you go again," said Jim, "defining what people should do before they even have time to feel out what is right for them. And it's always something that fits your view of people at the country club."

"Stop sneering," she said. "Those are fine people. And someday you'll want to belong to a club of your own. You certainly don't mind playing golf with them now."

"Dammit," he said, "I just want to do something meaningful with my life. Not just make a lot of money. Why can't you let me find my own way?"

In the meantime, Dad finished changing his clothes and came out of the bedroom. Maybe he could shed some light on this battle. So far he had stayed out of it. It was something between us boys and our mother. "What do you think, Dad?" I asked.

He looked into the fireplace for a minute, deliberately hitching his belt into the right notch. Then he turned to us who were more or less in a circle around the table. He made a pronouncement that I'll never forget. "I'll tell you what I think," he said. "I think you're all on the wrong track. Sure, I want you to be happy. And, sure, I want you to make a lot of money. And, sure, I want you to do what you like. But as for me, I don't give a damn what career you choose. All I care about is that you are always men of honor. I was thinking that at the courthouse the other day. I didn't like getting that call from the judge in the middle of the night saying that you were in trouble with the law. That's not my idea of what life is all about. So I'm glad that's all behind us now and you've learned from it. Do whatever you want to with your lives. I just want to know that you will always do what is right. That's what will make me proud."

No one could answer that. So we all turned with him and looked into the fire.

A Man Does What He Has to Do

Sometimes a person's conscience is fueled by a sense of duty that goes beyond the reasonable principles of justice and honor. For many people the meaning of life is to follow a moral code whose standards exceed both human law and common practice. My friend, Greg, struggled so over the love of a woman.

"I'll do it myself!" said Greg.

"But it's very difficult for a man to raise five kids alone, argued Diane. "Together we could raise your five and my two a lot easier."

"I know," he said. "But it wouldn't be right. I can't marry a divorced woman, and I certainly won't just live with one."

"Doesn't it count that we love each other?" she pleaded.

"Of course, it counts. But it doesn't make marriage morally right."

For ten years Greg had been married to Margaret. Beautiful Margaret. Dark hair, blue eyes, lovely complexion. Men envied his luck. They had five children—one every 18 to 24 months. Just the right pace for a couple following their church's teaching on birth control.

They had a happy life all those years, interrupted only by bouts of migraine headaches. Sometimes Margaret had to rest for several days in a dark room because her head hurt so much. Greg took over cooking, cleaning and washing the diapers. Fortunately, the factory let him adjust his hours on those days so he could be home when the older kids returned from school. He got to be a pretty good cook. The kids even preferred his spaghetti to Margaret's. This news made her smile. She said it was the reason why she had to get better and reclaim her place.

One morning the foreman called Greg into the office. "I just got a call from the hospital," he said gravely, "They said you should call. It's something about Margaret."

Greg called right away, reading the number from the small pink square of paper. When he hung up he said, "All they could tell me is that she has a very bad headache. They're doing some tests."

"That's too bad."

"I don't know what this means, but I'll probably need some extra time this afternoon. I hate to keep doing this to you, especially on a big production run."

"Has she ever gone to the hospital with this before?" asked the foreman.

"No, not just for a headache." Greg paused. "I don't know what to do. How about if I stayed till after the first run is finished? Then you could put Harriet on it."

"Think she'd go to the hospital if it wasn't serious?" asked the foreman again.

"No, you're right. Maybe I should go now. It's just that I feel responsible..." His voice trailed off.

"A guy has to do what he has to do," said the foreman.

Greg punched out and drove to the hospital. He was already too late. Almost to the minute on his time card she suffered a massive stroke. The weakened blood vessel which had caused so many headaches finally gave out completely. He held her hand for two hours and wept—until they gently pulled him away.

Diane was a neighbor. She and Margaret went shopping together and took the kids to the beach on sunny days. She knew and liked Greg's family. They liked her in return. When she divorced her husband because he was "never home," everyone was shocked. No one ever thought of her as having problems.

After Margaret died Diane kept Greg's family going. She brought supper. She invited them over. She arranged baby-sitters. She looked in on them long after the other neighbors went back to their normal routines.

"This past year I've come to love you," she told Greg. "And not just you, but all the kids. I feel like a second mother to them. I think we'd make a great blended family."

"It's all too convenient," said Greg. "But it's not *morally* right. I can't marry a divorced person. It's against everything I've been taught about right and wrong."

"You'd rather throw everything away for a moral principle that not everyone believes in?"

"I have to do what I believe is right," he said, "even though I know it's wrong."

In Greg's company are many persons who find meaning in strict adherence to a higher law. The test of their conviction comes when this law, as they understand it, does not conform to their reasonable desires. The meaning of their life is heroic obedience, knowing that they have lived up to their commitment in spite of the cost.

Questions for Reflection

When in your life did you struggle to do the right thing?

Do you try to live by a stricter code than your fellows? What is that code?

How often are you at the center of moral debates—about your own conduct? About that of others?

THE ROAD OF SALVATION

This is a good place to detour to the road of salvation. That's because it comes closest to the main road in the matter of morality—where human weakness is most apparent.

According to our map, two parallel roads run through the realms of Having, Doing and Being. Together they comprise a geography of the spirit. The main road, which we have been following, runs on the solid ground, but it is only open when we are at our best. The parallel road of salvation is narrow, crumbly and runs along a frightening precipice. It is the path we take when our own strength seems insufficient or life's dangers push us to the edge.

*What a wretched man I
am. Who will rescue
me from this body
doomed to death?*

Romans 7:24

BEING SAVED

Some of the dangers that make us yearn for salvation are tangible: cancer, alcoholism, depression, poverty, prejudice, abuse, torture or tyranny. Others are intangible: loneliness and alienation (in the realm of Having), failure, temptation and weakness (in the realm of Doing), and creaturely contingency (in the realm of Being). We all find ourselves on the road of salvation from time to time. That's because we are limited and vulnerable human beings. We occasionally need help to get back on the main road or to succeed in our projects.

But some fellow travelers find themselves frequently on the road of salvation. For them it is not a back road but the very way of life. They feel surrounded by insatiable desires, uncontrollable forces, enmities, frailties, compulsions, and corruption—what Tennessee Williams calls his "blue demons," or what others call the "nausea of life." Feeling out of control and over the edge, they call for help from a power greater than self.

For these, the meaning of life is the experience of constantly being saved by this benevolent power.

Lithium and the Lord

Denny called me one evening to share his gift of salvation. "I think God has finally brought it together for me," he said "That's why I want to invite you to a baptism."

Denny was my boyhood friend. We went to the same school. We fished together. We built a dormer on his house. We even did mischief together. I got in more trouble with Denny, especially when he got into one of his excited moods. One night we threw tomatoes at a bus and overturned some garbage cans. Once we shot a marble out of a pipe with a cherry bomb and blew a hole in the neighbor's garage. Another time a policeman caught us with cigarettes and drove us home in a squad car. Experiences like that bound us for life.

So I was happy when Denny announced that his life had turned around. He said the Lord had saved him from his moodiness. He remembered with regret the time when, as a young labor negotiator, he un-wrapped a dead fish to show the union's reaction to management's proposal. He was also going to quit his present job because his boss emphasized profits at the expense of customer service. He realized how much he himself had caused the divorce with his first wife and how blessed he was to have found Charlene and her two daughters. And now he had a son of his own. He felt whole again, and it was time to put his family in the hands of God.

He celebrated the baptism in his home. The pastor came to sanction the event, but Denny conducted it himself. First he declared his own repentance. Then he poured the water over all three children. He cupped the water out of a crystal bowl that was a family heirloom. His brothers and sister recalled stories from the bad times and declared with tears the joy they felt now. My wife and I and a doctor friend were the sponsors. Denny's mother beamed as she put the white garments she had sewn on each of the children. We feasted on prime rib and celebrated into the night.

Soon thereafter Denny moved his family to the Carolina seaboard and opened an elegant restaurant flanked by specialty shops. His father-in-law, a wealthy race horse owner and Triple Crown contender, helped finance the venture. It was a whole new life for them. A family business. A new beginning. Denny worked tirelessly to build the structure, organize the business and find clientele among the yacht owners, vacationers and local people. Charlene ran the shops and did the book work. Her mother chose the decorations and selected the menus. They build a home next door. Every Sunday they went to church.

Then one summer Denny's moods started to return. He worked all the harder to force them away, but the strain showed. His forehead tensed in a scowl. He snapped at the staff. "Oh please, Denny," begged Charlene, "please see a doctor." Finally he agreed.

"I believe it's manic depression," explained the doctor. He tried to be reassuring, but the news was stunning. "It's caused by a chemical imbalance, usually inherited. There's really nothing to worry about. Ninety-five percent of the time we can handle it with medication. This prescription for lithium should keep the balance steady. These other two prescriptions are meant to soften the peaks. They should be taken rarely—only if you go to an extreme high or low."

The lithium worked for several years. During this time they visited us. Their son was grown up enough to play with our kids. This was something Denny had looked forward to, so his lack of animation was surprising. We asked if something was wrong. That's when they explained.

A lot of things fell into place. Why Denny was sometimes so excited as a kid and got us into trouble. Why he was sometimes withdrawn and hard to play with. And why his father was so erratic. We were all a little frightened of his father when he got in one of his "moods."

"I'm afraid that's what's happening to me," said Denny.

"What's saving us now," said Charlene, "is lithium and the Lord."

"I don't have to use the uppers or downers too much," Denny added. "I hate to use any medicine at all."

Over the next few months Denny started to need his medicines more and more. The lows got lower and the highs got higher. One time he fired the head waiter just for coming in late. And then he re-hired the man the next day in a spirit of compunction.

"I'm no good to you any more," he said one night to Charlene. "I'm worse than my father. I don't deserve to be part of this family. All we've built here is for nothing."

"Oh, Denny," she pleaded, "please hang on. We love you so much. The bad times go away. We can wait them out with God's help. And sometimes we are so much at peace."

The peaceful times became less frequent. They cherished them with hugs and celebrations. The business was doing well, so they hired a manager to give them more time to enjoy their periods of well being. The manager also freed them to work out of the bad times. More than once Denny was hospitalized to get stable, and occasionally to detox from a desperate overdose.

"This can't go on," Denny said in a particularly black spell. "I'm no good to you." One time Charlene was horrified to find a pistol in Denny's drawer. She threw out the bullets and buried the gun in the back yard. Another time she opened the family album and found holes in the photographs. Denny had cut his image out of the pictures. One day she found his wedding ring in the jewelry box. It had been flattened with a hammer.

"Oh, God, we need your help," she cried.

In the late Spring the weather turned foul. It rained for three days and Denny became increasingly irritable. Charlene felt him get up in the middle of the night, but she was too exhausted to protest. The next morning the van was gone. So were all his pills. She drove around the town looking for him. She called his mother in Minneapolis. Once before he had driven all that way in a frantic urge to go somewhere safe.

The sheriff called on the third day. They had found the van. It was mired in a dirt road up the coast. The radio was on and the battery run down. The pill bottles lay open around Denny's body. Only a few of the downers remained. An autopsy confirmed the overdose. The note he left said simply: "Lord, save me. I don't know what else to do."

Because I was an old friend, the family asked me to say a few words at the funeral. What do you say about a suicide? I talked about the good things he had done, the sincerity of his struggles, and his eagerness to be saved. "He believed fervently in the gift of saving grace," I concluded. "Let us choose to believe that he received it."

One Day at a Time

This next story is about salvation fulfilled. It's about depending on a Higher Power for every minute of precious sobriety. It's my mother-in-law's story.

Mae was already sitting in a booth by the front window when Marge entered the cafe.

"Nice to see you, Mae," said Marge. "Sorry if I'm a little late. I had to drive Bud to the barber shop on the way over. His arthritis is acting up again."

"Oh, I'm sorry."

"Thanks. It's not too bad. But I'll have to pick him up on the way home too."

"Of course. Don't give it another thought. Can he take care of himself for that long?"

"Oh, he'll be fine. He'll read the paper and talk with the boys. How's John?"

"Gettin' along. " Mae paused, knowing this was not the whole truth. "Actually, he's drinking again. There was most of a quart gone this morning, and we served only a little to guests yesterday."

"Well, there's nothing you can do about it, you know."

"I know: 'Accept the things I cannot change,'" she recited. "It's just so hard sometimes."

"One day at a time, my friend," said Marge.

Marge and Mae often met on their way to AA meetings. Marge was Mae's sponsor. She brought her into the program ten years before. Mae had been a binge drinker. She would go several months without a drink. Then, usually with the let down after a big family event, she would start to drink wine. A little at first. Then more. Finally she took the bottle to bed with her. She emerged every so often, disheveled and dressed in a bathrobe. Her mood was ugly and irritable. "I was usually such a nice person", she said once at a meeting, "but drink let me assert myself. I'd even snap at my husband who ordinarily took no guff from me." Then after three or four days she slept it off, wept with remorse and returned to normal.

John, by contrast, drank all the time. He was a lifelong alcoholic who needed a drink just to keep going. In fact, he seemed to function better with a drink than without it. He only swore off when drinking got him in trouble or when the doctor insisted on it. He had been on a long "dry". Now he was drinking again. Mae needed somebody.

"I'm glad you're my sponsor," Mae said. "You're always so calm and caring."

"Well, you're a person worth caring about," Marge replied.

"It took a lot of caring to get me here. I sure didn't care for myself in those drinking days."

Mae remembered the time her daughter brought an AA friend home to invite her into the program. "I listened politely. And though I was in an awful mess, my pride wouldn't let me admit it. Later the friend told Maureen that I just wasn't bad enough. Boy did that make her mad—at me, at her friend, and at God."

"I just remember the time we came to get you," said Marge. "You must have been ready then. You came willingly enough."

"Yes," Mae said recalling. "It was about a year later. I had invited Maureen's other friend Margaret over for dinner. The table was set and everything was ready. You know how I love to prepare for a dinner party. Everything just right. I only had to put the roast in the oven and boil the potatoes. The rest was in the refrigerator, including my Waldorf salad."

"You make a great Waldorf," Marge couldn't help interjecting.

"I thought I would just have a little glass of wine. To relax. Did I ever relax! When Margaret arrived the jug was half gone, I was still in my housecoat, and the meat was sitting raw on the kitchen counter. When Johnny got home a few minutes later, all hell broke loose. Called me a 'dumb broad' and every other name in the book. Me, who put up with all *his* episodes!" She stopped and took a breath to shake off the flare of resentment. "Anyway, after he stormed out Margaret convinced me to call Maureen's AA friend again. That's when you came in the picture."

"Well, I'm sure glad you called. The program has saved so many of us. I wasn't always sober myself, you know."

"I know," said Mae. "I only wish it could save Johnny too."

"Maybe someday it will. When he is ready. It's there for anyone who wants to change."

"I guess he isn't bad enough yet."

"Does that make you mad at him—and at God?"

"I see what you mean," said Mae, struck with guilt that she might be angry with God. "I guess I just have to put him in God's hands and take it one day at a time."

They paid for the coffee and got up to leave for the meeting. As they started for the door, Mae added, "Thank God for one day at a time."

An *"Ave"* for First Base

My own experience of salvation is more episodic. It comes and goes with burning insights into my own fragility. It peaked when I was twelve years old.

I wanted nothing more than to play baseball on St. Bernard School's varsity team. What other payoff was there for the thousands of hours we practiced in the sandlot next to our house? What better recompense to Marty and Gerta who lived on the other side for the broken windows and scuffed siding?

At the same time I was an altar boy at the church. One of my duties was to serve at special novenas, rosaries and stations of the cross. The best job was thurifer. That's the one who carries the censor and incense boat. The next best job was bell ringer. The third boy just knelt on the other side—seemingly for ballast.

As the baseball trials approached, I got particularly pious. The evening before, I came early to the rosary devotions. I let someone else be thurifer. All my energy was focused on praying to win the first base spot on the team. I settled for bell ringer. We processed to the altar of the Blessed Virgin, in front of a statue whose eyes regarded us with deep compassion. We started to pray.

"Hail Mary ... help me make the team. Blessed art thou among women ... if anyone can help, you can. Blessed is the fruit of thy womb, Jesus ... ask him to help me, too. Pray for us sinners ... yes, but I'm terribly sorry. Can't I play first base?"

Next day the try-outs took place after supper at Lawson Playground. First Mr. Tschida, the coach, had us catch some flies. We all charged the ball, eager to show our zeal and prowess. I jumped up and snagged a one-hander with my trusty wide-mouthed glove. Oh, this was going to be the day that the Lord has blessed.

Then he called in those who wanted to try out for the infield. There were a lot of kids for shortstop and only a few less for second and third. All right-handers. There were just me and one right-handed kid going for first. Being left-handed, I felt sure of getting the nod. "Oh thank you, God, for making me left-handed like Lou Gehrig."

My turn was first, and I ran to the coveted post. Mr. Tschida was hitting hot grounders. Crack! Down to third base.

117

The guys were scooping them up and firing to first. I leaned out to grab the ball way before it got to the bag. Crack to short and over to first. We were getting this rhythm down. I was in on every play. I'd scoop the ball and toss it deftly to Mr. Tschida at the plate. Crack to second and over to first. Toss to the coach. We were already a smooth running team.

Crack to first! It was going to be a two-hopper. Too short to get on the first bounce. Everything hung on the second bounce, which was going to be just in front of my feet. I aimed the wide-open, left-handed glove.

I don't know how I missed the ball. Maybe it hit a pebble. But it slipped behind the glove and struck me in the groin. Crack! Down at first!

I remember Mr. Tschida looking down at me. Such pity I never wanted to see, not even in the eyes of the Blessed Virgin. He bent over and pulled on my belt to help me breathe. My brother assisted me to the bench. This was not the salvation I was looking for. I went behind the bleachers and tossed my supper. Between the slats I saw Mr. Tschida hitting more grounders to the infielders. It seemed like he wasn't hitting them as hard as before. The right-handed kid was at first. They had a pretty good rhythm going.

The team roster was posted a few days later. I looked at it with some hope. But I wasn't surprised when my name wasn't on the list. I didn't quit the altar boys, but I never prayed for anything specific again—only for the strength to stay on the main road.

"Now and at the hour of our death. Amen."

Questions for Reflection

Recall an event in which you felt lost, incomplete or abandoned. What saved you? How did you feel?

Name the dark forces you can't control in your life—the sins, addictions, and hurts from the past. How important is it to be free of them?

What power do you rely on when nothing else works?

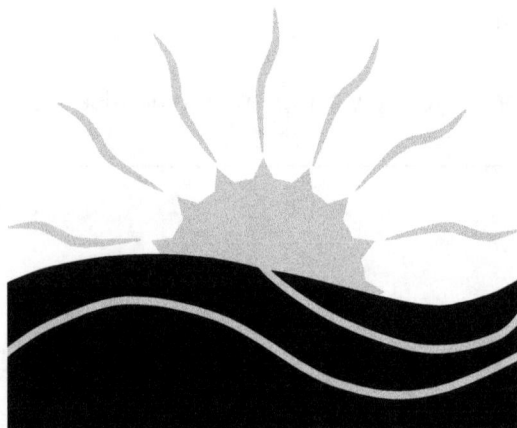

THE REALM OF BEING

We come at last to the Realm of Being. It is the third of three great areas where people find meaning. It lies near the top of the world, beyond the familiar realms of Having and Doing. The narrow entry requires leaving much baggage behind. Once inside, the realm opens to a vast expanse of natural beauty filled with deep rivers, enchanted forests, boundless oceans, brooding mountains and searing deserts. Here and there we see condensed outposts of civilization— libraries, universities, monasteries and sanctuaries.

The inhabitants are saints, scholars, scientists, mystics and poets. And surprisingly many ordinary people—people who like to read, to garden and to pray. People perhaps like you.

The road itself is hard to discern, less trodden as it is. Sometimes it's a mere path in the woods or a blurred footprint in the sand. The terrain is wildly expansive, unrolling to infinity. We will begin at the narrow end where we can still focus on individual beings. Then we will see how Being expands enormously and even dangerously through knowledge, change and communion until it disappears in a mystery of transcendence. More than anywhere, meaning here consists in giving oneself *literally* to what is greater than self.

So let's stay close together as we step into this awesome and holy place.

*People say that what
we're all seeking is a
meaning for life. ...
I think what we're really
seeking is an intense
experience of being alive.*

Joseph Campbell

BEING PRESENT IN THE WORLD

Our first stop in the Realm of Being is surprisingly noisy and crude. It's not the quiet library or hermitage we might have expected. It looks more like a big dance hall, and the people inside are waving their arms, shouting gleefully, and thoroughly enjoying each other.

Presence as a form of meaning is not highly refined or intellectual. It is a gut-level appreciation of just being there. It is *being* in its rawest form—a kind of amazement that I am present with other beings, especially other human beings. It's a joyous celebration of sheer existence.

Here I Am!

When I was just old enough to talk, my parents liked to play a game with me. They would set me in my high chair and look me in the face. Then they would glance over my head or around the room pretending not to see me. "Where's Tommy?" they would ask. "I don't see him." And the other would say, "I don't see him either. Where is he?" I would wave my arms wildly to get their attention and shout, "Hee I iss! Hee I iss!" Then suddenly discovering me, they would say, "Oh, *there* he is!" And we would all laugh and giggle.

That's the way it is with presence. Its meaning is this awesome but joyful sense that I am here with you. You can pretend not to see me sometimes. You can get caught up with other things that seem more important. I can get caught up with them too. But sometimes I realize that I am here with all these wonderful powers of a conscious being—powers of knowing, appreciating, changing and interacting.

Why Not Nothing?

Part of the meaning comes from realizing that we don't have to be. The millions of bits of genetic material that swirled through history into our unique combination could have done otherwise. That we have any being at all is an incredible coincidence. As Ray Nogar says in *Lord of the Absurd*, "The real question is: Why not nothing? The awareness of contingency [gives you] the queasy feeling that your existence is leaning hard on nothing." Living in a world with over a billion other people sometimes makes us forget the sheer wonder of our existence. Those who savor presence as a form of meaning are happy to get up every morning and just say: "Here I am! Wow!" Theirs is a feeling of profound gratitude for just being.

Though this form of meaning is not difficult to grasp, it is easy to take for granted. Most of us lose sight of it in our pursuit of having, doing or other forms of meaning. Sometimes it takes a dramatic experience to make us appreciate it.

Enough to Be Alive

Lil is a woman of strong opinions, and vigorous action. She raised three daughters in accord with her beliefs. She made sure they were well educated. She urged them to march for political causes. She drafted them to work in soup kitchens and clothing drives.

She wanted so much for them. One daughter was a natural actress, and Lil was proud to see her talent shine in community theater. Another was a dancer—athletic, buoyant and full of promise. The third was a sweet girl, withdrawn and obese. It was a struggle to draw her out, build up her self esteem and engage her in outgoing activities. Lil did what each one needed to be their best.

Then the telephone rang. The telephone will never sound friendly to Lil again. It was about Cathy, the dancer. "Your daughter was struck by an automobile," the voice said. "Virtually every bone in her body is broken. If she lives, I'm sorry to say, she will never dance again."

Well, it turned out she lived. The family pulled together in anxious vigil. They hoped and prayed through intensive care. They waited agonizing hours for the vital signs to stabilize. Days more to know if her kidneys would recuperate. Then weeks to know if her limbs could be saved. Then months to know if she would walk again. Hours and hours of therapy.

Finally, she came home. Little by little she learned to walk. One day the feeling returned to her toes. And then the strength. And then—one morning—the dancing.

"Oh, Lil," I said, "What you've been through. How proud you must be!"

"No," she said with great conviction. "It's not really pride. It's something else. I used to want so much for my children. I wanted them to lead such meaningful lives. But I've changed my mind. Now it's just enough that they're alive."

When you appreciate the meaning of presence, nothing else matters. You don't have to have anything. You don't have to do anything. You just have to be. This realization brings a great sense of peace.

Prolonging the Peace

Bill was my best friend in Germany. We were both students at the University of Tuebingen. While I was polishing bathtubs for a tiny room at Frau Beuchler's, he was enjoying a whole apartment to himself. He loved the view from his balcony: the golden castle floating above the deep green of the Nekkar valley. He could look at it for hours. He was also the only person I knew who liked to meditate with his head down and his feet up.

One Saturday morning I stopped by to have him read something I was writing. He had promised to be home, so I was surprised when no one answered the bell. I rang and rang. Still no answer. I walked around to the side under the balcony. Not seeing him, I threw pebbles at the second-story window. Nothing. When I returned to the door, the landlady came out and asked what was going on.

"Herr Wilhelm," I muttered. "Isn't he home?"

"Ja, Ja," she said, "I heard the water running a while ago and he hasn't come down."

Finally, he appeared in the stairway. "Oh, you're here," he said with surprise. "Come on up."

"I've been ringing and ringing," I chided. "Where have you been?"

"I was meditating. I guess I didn't hear you."

"You mean you've been standing on your head again," I said too severely, "and it's finally mushed your brains."

He reddened a little but kept his calm. "No, not this time. But I do go into myself when I meditate."

Most of us just catch glimpses of presence and its undisturbed peace in the spaces between our regular consciousness. Real devotees, like Bill, refine and prolong the experience through yoga and meditation. They get themselves into an altered state of consciousness where nothing else concerns them. They quiet their senses and even their thoughts to focus on the pure experience of being. Personally, I am satisfied with a small diet of these experiences. My friend Bill literally turned his life upside down for them.

A Kind of Existentialism

Some people call this feeling of presence "existentialism." I suppose it is, though of a very medieval sort—you know, monks with skulls on their desks, contemplating the shortness and precariousness of existence. Mainstream existentialists like Kierkegaard, Sartre and Camus are more concerned about what we *do* with our existence, a view that we will examine in the chapter on becoming.*

So it's interesting that Sartre's intimate companion, Simone de Beauvoir, describes the meaning of her own mother's life in terms of a devotion to sheer existence. Nothing else that the mother dedicated her life to—neither order, nor morality, nor family love, nor religious tradition—was more important in the final hours. Here is how de Beauvoir tells about her vigil:

> I was sitting on the bed watching the feeble breathing raise and lower ever so slightly the black cord of the locket on her blouse. She opened her eyelids around six in the evening.
>
> "What time is it? I don't understand. Is it night already?"
>
> "You've slept all afternoon," I said.
>
> "I've slept forty-eight hours?"

---

* A group of modern existentialists who describe being as a sense of presence include Jacques Maritain and Etienne Gilson. Heidegger's "Dasein" (being there) also bears this connotation to some degree.

"No, of course not." I reminded her about earlier events, how she had suffered so from the cancer and been given a shot of morphine.

"Ah yes," she said with reproach. "But I am losing days. Today I hardly lived at all." For her, each day had irreplaceable value. She regretted the loss of even a few hours.

After a few spoonfuls of soup we talked about my sister coming to spend the night. Who would stay and for how long. "It's all the same to me," she said. And after a moment of reflection she added, "What bothers me the most is that nothing bothers me. It's all the same to me."

When I came back the next afternoon she was sleeping and Chantal was sitting on the bed. "Poor Chantal," Mama said later. "She has so much to do and I take up her time."

"But it pleases her," I said. "She loves you so much."

Mama thought about that for a while then in a surprised and heart-broken voice she said, "I don't know if I love anyone any more."

This declaration of indifference struck me deeply. I compared it to what she had said so often earlier when she saw how many people had come to visit her. She had said with so much pride, "They like to visit me because I'm cheerful." Little by little people had lost their importance for her. Now her heart was empty, drained by the fatigue of dying.

It surprised us that so pious a woman never asked for a priest. She never took out the missal, crucifix or rosary that Martha had brought to the hospital. One morning Jean suggested, "It's Sunday, Aunt Francoise, wouldn't you like to take communion?"

"Oh dear no," she replied. "I'm too tired to pray. Besides, God is good." Later when someone asked if she wanted a confessor, her face hardened and she said, "Too tired" and closed her eyes to end the conversation.

128

We know that religion was the pivot and substance of her whole life. All the papers we found in her desk afterward confirmed that. Yet in the end all she wanted was to live. When my grandmother died, she talked about going to join her husband, Gustave. My father showed no less courage in accepting the ruin and end of his life. But Mama revolted against it. Not even religion gave her hope of a posthumous victory. No heavenly immortality nor earthly monument can console you in the face of death when you cling to life as much as she.

Simone de Beauvoir, Une mort tres douce,
Gallimard, 1964. Author's translation, edited.

In the end, when trouble comes, the world ignores us, things get boring, or maybe even God seems not to notice— those who find their deepest meaning in the wonder of personal presence, clap their hands and shout however feebly, "Hee I iss, world, hee I iss!"

Questions for Reflection

Has any loss, misfortune or near miss caused you to deeply appreciate the marvel of your existence?

In what ways are you amazed at the unique combination of powers, talents and circumstance that you were born with?

To what degree are you at peace just to be alive?

*Let us bring our minds to
rest in the glory of the
Divine Truth. May Truth
inspire our reflection.*

Rig Veda III,62,10

KNOWING AND SHARING THE TRUTH

Our journey through the Realm of Being takes us to ever more challenging places. We leave behind the noisy and sociable borderlands where it is relatively easy to appreciate being in its raw state. Mounting a bank of white marble stairs, we enter a quiet green quadrangle surrounded by great ivied halls. The imposing facades of libraries, laboratories, and lecture halls announce a new and more demanding kind of being. The people here have a studious, disciplined look. They often sit alone under a tree reading. Through the windows we see them logged onto the Internet. When they speak, it's one at a time. Their intensity betrays the presence of a fascinating unseen world, the world of *being as known.*

What impresses these scholars is the gigantic *expansion of being* that takes place in human knowledge. They realize that their personal being is but a vessel that contains a whole world of other beings. Through knowledge, says Aristotle, "the soul is in a way all existing things." This wonderful new dimension of being is what the philosophers call "cognitive being"—the being of the other as other and yet in me. Everything becomes an object of my knowledge, something I carry with me *inside my being* even when my hands are empty.

Keeping the Truth Alive

We all delight in knowing things. But those who find a special meaning in knowledge do not just enjoy it as a passing interest. They dedicate themselves to a "body" of knowledge—knowing as much as possible about it, mastering it, evolving it, keeping it alive, as it were, in their own being.

Some are masters of baseball statistics. Others know a lot about money, real estate, types of dogs, and World War II airplanes. My friend Jack knows every detail about Studebaker automobiles. My own son can name the make, model and engine specifications of every car we pass on the highway. I don't know how he gets all that information, certainly not from me. My dad loves history. Another friend pores over the New York Times and can tell you anything about current books, songs and plays.

The real champions of knowledge, however, don't just know a lot of information. They care about something greater than that—a fragile universe of being, called "Truth," whose very existence consists in human research and dialogue. For these, the meaning of life is to keep the truth alive and up to date.

The Passion of Science

Bob knows a lot about birds. My kids watched him one morning on a children's science program. The show came on at 7:30 on the public TV channel. The kids liked to watch it before going to school. So thirsty were their minds for knowledge. Neither did I refrain from peering over their shoulders while I knotted my tie.

Bob works from grant to grant—for whoever funds his pursuit of knowledge about birds. "We're tracking the painted bunting today," he intoned as the camera crew descended from the Jeep to his camp. "The painted bunting is closely related to the sparrow. Did you know that the American tree sparrow is really a bunting? The painted bunting is easy to spot because it's the only bird in the world with a blue head and red under parts. The female is a brilliant yellow green. This one is a male. See the red feathers under the bill?"

He let the male go and took a female from a big trapping net slung down from a tree. He gently calmed the bird and put a band around its leg. "We're trying to find out how they know where to fly when they migrate. These bands tell us how many have been to the same place more than once. It's patient work, but it really pays off. If we keep at it, some day we'll know more about nature and why these beautiful creatures do what they do."

Bob is a scientist, an ornithologist. His meaning is bound up with knowing the truth about his special science. And yet it is a form of meaning that he will share with anyone who listens. A feature of knowledge is that we can all share it without cutting it up or fighting for possession. As Larry Wilson once said, "If I share a dollar with you, we each have half a dollar. If I share an idea with you, we both have a whole idea."

And so Bob is eager not only to refine his knowledge but to pass it on—to expand his being and yours at the same time.

Seeing the Big Picture

There is a special kind of meaning that comes from considering truth in its widest possible context. It consists in seeing the big picture—how the world hangs together, not just in this or that science, but in its entire wholeness.

In my first year of college, I read an article in the Saturday Evening Post about the Dominicans, the great Order of

Preachers dedicated to the pursuit of truth. I liked their motto: "To contemplate and to give to others the fruit of one's contemplation." Imagine, I thought, a worldwide brotherhood dedicated to so lofty an idea.

I joined and went through a boot camp called the novitiate. It was located on a high bluff over the Mississippi. The initiation consisted of chanting the Psalms hour after hour, verse by verse from alternating sides of the choir. Repetition and reverence were the foundation of the promised contemplation. The steady tone of the chant opened a great space in my mind, like a huge canvas, that cried out to be filled by the grandest thoughts of the masters.

They sent me next to Chicago for a long course of study. First came logic and much practice in constructing complex arguments. I took my turn defending a thesis in Latin in a public debate, called a "disputatio." This was a tradition inherited from the medieval schools, not unlike the famous debate between Martin Luther and Johann Eck. I sat on a raised platform under the Gothic arches of the monastery's common room in front of the entire community. We were all clad in white robes and black capes.

"Greetings to the reverend fathers, to my dear brothers and to the entire array of listeners," I began nervously the ritual introduction. "The thesis to be defended today is ..." I stated my well-rehearsed arguments, bringing to bear as many connections as I could muster on the truth of my proposition.

When I finished, a hefty faculty member named John Bonnet, who was as nimble in Latin as Eck himself, rose to make the objections. This was the really terrifying part, especially since I could tell from the twinkle in his eye that he was just playing with me. But I answered all his objections with some semblance of logic and ended with a confident declaration of victory, "*quod erat demonstrandum.*"

I don't know if I really won, but I felt like I had thrown a touchdown pass in a college football game. I could tell that I was going to like this kind of meaning. There was something exciting about this "contemplation."

There followed many years of studying the great works of philosophy and theology. I began to see connections between all the parts of knowledge and the different kinds of knowledge. I began to understand why logic was so important—because it is needed to sort out contending views about the really big picture. For example, it makes a difference to the meaning of the picture:

- Whether you think that everything evolves to a greater state, or is just a pile of dust particles knocking together;

- Whether you think that human being has a special place in the structure of things, or is just a bundle of desires lost in a small outpost of the universe;

- Whether you think that all being is charged with consciousness and love, or just so-many blind mechanisms that flash today and burn themselves out;

- Whether you think that there is a unifying world principle that shouldn't be violated, or just a bunch of stuff we can use for one moment and discard the next.

Questions like these led eventually to the consideration of being as such—being as *being.* This was finally what they meant by contemplation: to consider and appreciate the qualities of all being—its dynamism, its beauty, its goodness, and indeed, its truth.

I don't know whether I ever reached the heights of contemplation envisioned by my teachers. But I do understand the tremendous sense of meaning that they were pointing to—perhaps impossible to achieve and lost in mystery, but wonderfully attractive nonetheless—namely, being able to know the furthest reaches of being in a way that really savors its vitality, goodness and truth.

After finishing my studies I taught college philosophy with the Dominicans for a number of years. It was my way to give to others the fruits of so much contemplation. I could tell right away in the classroom that not everyone shared my passion. Many students liked to learn, but only a few had that spark, that desire to see the big picture—to understand things, as Aristotle says, "in terms of their first causes and principles."

Truth in the Mud

Yet, I am always looking for people with that spark—even in the strangest places. Here's a meeting that took place on a motorcycle/camping trip I took down the coast of Yugoslavia many years before that country broke up in a bloody war. It was a moment of recognition between two scholars a world and a generation apart.

It had been raining for three days and I was cold and miserable. The road had just been cut through the mountains south of Dubrovnik and every so often I had to steer around a huge boulder in the middle of the pavement. There was no use camping, so I stayed in cheap hotels and spread my soggy tent, towels and sleeping bag all over the room and halls to dry. I made sure my books were double-wrapped in plastic bags.

At noon on the third day I turned off the main highway into the muddy village of Kasousta Mitrovica. The water-stained houses hardly contrasted with the dark unpaved streets and the dull gray skies. I found a small bakery on the main street. The baker and his wife worked at an open-faced stone oven behind a huge wooden table. I purchased a loaf of bread and stayed inside to eat some. It was the first time I felt warm all day.

When I got outside about thirty school children were standing around my bike. They were all smiling and curious. I let them touch it while I stashed the rest of the loaf in one of my saddlebags.

"Do you speak English?" a tiny voice inquired.

"Yes," I replied to the lovely ten year old girl who asked. "My name is Tom. What is your name?"

"Krisna", she said. She was clutching five or six books in front of her.

"I see you have a lot of books, Krisna. So do I. But they are all wrapped up in my luggage."

"Yes," she said showing me her little library. "I have a book of geography, and one of English stories. Here is one on science. This one is Yugoslav history."

"Do you like to study?"

"Yes. I want to know about the truth."

The truth, I thought, yes, that is what we scholars seek. Then feeling the other kids' presence, I said, "Your English is good, Krisna. Will you translate for me? Will you say hello to all your friends?" At that she blushed, shook her head and retreated into the crowd. Public speaking was apparently not one of her talents. I started the motor and all the children stepped back.

"Dovidenja," I shouted. It was the only greeting I knew in their language. I don't know if it means hello or good-bye or something else. But they all shouted it back eagerly enough. As I got on, I noticed that Krisna had stepped to the front of the crowd again.

"Good-bye, Krisna. Study hard if you want to know the truth."

"Yes," she said, "I promise."

I hope, of course, that she has been untouched by the recent war in her country. But I hope even more that she kept her promise and that she is pursuing the truth. And if so, I wonder how far she is letting her mind expand: to data, to art, to science, to invention—to the very truth of being?

Questions for Reflection

How much of the world do you hold in your mind? How much of it has come into being only because of your thinking?

What important truth have you discovered? Have you passed it on to others?

How big is your picture of the world? How important is it to know how it fits together?

Who among your friends pursues this form of meaning?

Be all you can be.

US Army

BECOMING AN EVER-GREATER SELF

Leaving the difficult yet civilized halls of knowledge, we pass through an enchanted forest that presents a more threatening part of the Realm of Being. Its many paths start out well-marked, then diverge and disappear. It is easy to get lost here. From the shadows we hear eerie voices calling us to a scary transformation. We catch glimpses of dark, dreamlike creatures who claim to be our very selves—gnomes, warriors, tricksters, waifs and magicians who rise like vapor from our collective unconscious.

In the center of the forest is a way station, not unlike King Arthur's court. It is a place of deep reflection and soul-searching. The travelers who rest here have a strong and healthy look, but they say little, as if trying to absorb some new experience that has shaken their being to the core.

This is the place of becoming. Becoming is what happens to us when we plunge eagerly into life and discover that we have changed along the way. We might describe it as a lifelong accumulation of qualities, experiences and identities. The *meaning* of becoming is to discover that one's being is richer and deeper for having changed.

Becoming is another *expansion* of being. It's not the expansion of knowledge that comes from packing a lot of cognitive being into one's regular being. It's an expansion of one's very *self*. It's like the molting of a butterfly—"I am still me, but I am more."

This is what the existentialists refer to when they say that essence comes after existence. "That" we are is just a fact. "Who" we are is something we become—mostly by choice but also by the sheer absorption of experience. Those who find special meaning here consider their personal being to be a work of art that takes a lifetime to finish.

Becoming through Commitment

The choices we make to expand our being usually take the form of commitments. My wife is good at this. Early in our marriage we did not have a dog. That's because of my childhood experience with Bambi. Bambi was a five year old cocker spaniel that Dad brought home because one of his clients was getting too old to care for it. At first my brother and I were thrilled—though Bambi obviously was not. He barked and whined continuously. In spite of all our attention he kept snapping at us and trying to run away. In desperation, we put him in the basement, which he proceeded to fill with excrement. Finally, one day he ran away for good. I cried but I was glad too.

Years later my new bride announced that she wanted us to get a dog. She had grown up with many dogs and couldn't wait to get one. "Now that we have a house," she said, "it's time to get a dog."

"No!" I exclaimed in horror. "The last thing I want is a dog."

"Why not?" she asked.

"Because they bark and smell and poop and jump all over you. I can't stand the idea of one leaping on me and exhaling dog-breath in my face and licking my lips. The very sight of one in the kitchen makes me want to throw up."

She argued for a long time, told me how nice they really were, and tried to coax me out of my irrational distaste.

"No," I said with absolute resolve. "I'd rather give up our house or our marriage than live with a dog!" This was the end of the conversation. She turned away sullen and disappointed.

A few days later she spoke to me again with tears in her eyes. "I've been thinking about the dog," she said, "and I've made up my mind that I can't be myself if you command what we have and what we do. I can't let you win and me lose. And yet I love you and commit myself to being your wife. So I've decided to make you a gift. And the gift is that I shall stop wanting a dog."

Now it was my turn to weep. She knew how to make a commitment—how to change who she was without changing who she really was.

We all have an evolving identity. It is human nature to be an unfinished product until the moment we die—and then, who knows how much more we change. But the person who finds great meaning in this evolution does not just endure it or go along with it. She chooses it. She makes it her aim to *incorporate new identities* through a series of commitments.

An Eagle Scout of Meaning

Jim is another of those courageous, existential travelers. He was my college roommate. I've watched him transform his being many times over the years.

In the early days he was simply a jock. Everything was achievement and winning. Sports consumed his life—and our room in the dormitory.

"God, it stinks in here," I'd say.

"Yeah?   Well your pipe smells worse than my gym clothes."

"No, way! One whiff of your sweaty pants is worth two pounds of tobacco."

We decided we deserved each other and agreed not to complain about the odors. Still the best day was Thursday, when we walked downtown and did the laundry.

After college Jim became an artist, intent on creating beauty. He played the guitar in graduate school and led evening song sessions on the front steps of the nursing school dorm. One time we went on a canoe trip in the Boundary Waters Canoe Area. While the rest of us were reading or cleaning fish, he would sit on a rocky point and sketch the sunset.

After graduate school he worked briefly in a community center. He returned to school to pursue knowledge as a form of meaning. He chose to teach in a college where his quick insight and passionate rhetoric made him one of the most popular teachers.

In another phase, he took a stand for social justice. He urged the business people attending his lectures to change the structures of society that oppress the poor.

One day he said, "I'm moving into a tenement in the immigrant neighborhood."

"Why?" we asked.

"So I can be one with them. Today I met a woman who said there were rats in her apartment. I need to see this for myself. I will work with the poor to change society."

"You can do that from here," we protested.

"No, I have to go there and be their friend."

He gave up all but a few hours of his regular work in order to have very little money. And he spent several years visiting people, fixing their plumbing, exterminating rats, and strengthening porch railings so kids would have a safe place to play.

He never married for many years. Then he fell in love and changed again. At the present time he is married and seems to be pursuing family love as a form of meaning.

Jim is one of those travelers who seeks a fullness of being that comes from taking on many new commitments. He is like an Eagle Scout who gains life's merit badges, one after another. If you look in a scout handbook you will find the badges that apply: art, athletics, canoeing, communication, home repair, nature, music, public speaking, scholarship, plumbing, hiking, and citizenship. When he dies, I picture a sash with all these badges laid across his coffin. I also picture a strange multitude at the funeral: family in front, students on one side, business men on the other, and immigrants by the door—all giving homage to this man of many identities.

Stretching Your Being

When I ask, most people over thirty say that "having children" or "being a parent" is the most significant event of their lives. Prodded to explain, they talk for a while about the wonder of procreation, the excitement of giving birth, and the joy of bringing home this tiny bundle who looks like themselves. But after a few minutes of delightful reminiscence, they often come to the real point—having children has committed them to become many things they otherwise would not have become.

Here is how one couple, Jan and Tony, described it:

Tony: After we got married we both worked for a year to get established. We didn't think about having a family until we got a house and some of the things we always wanted.

Jan: I remember one Sunday in the Fall how wonderful it was to tramp in the leaves and buy apples at a roadside stand. We came home to our new house, made a fire and cooked cheese fondue right there on our hearth.

Tony: We both had good jobs, careers actually, in which we were making a contribution and exercising leadership. Jan was still finishing college, and I needed to get my fill of playing in a rock band.

Jan: We were also active in our church—we still are—and we had a lot of friends. We did a lot of visiting in those days.

Tony: Then one day she says, "Our life isn't big enough. Let's have a baby." I said, "Why?" And she said, "I don't feel stretched enough, and the house has more space than we need." I suggested that we take in a boarder. But she meant growing in a deeper way.

Jan: Boy, did I find out. Having two kids has stretched me every possible way—physically and mentally. I'm not my old self anymore. I keep being forced to become new people: mother, nursemaid, teacher, pet-doctor, chauffeur, referee... One thing after another. And Tony too, he ...

Tony: I don't feel it has changed my job so much. I still spend most of my days at work. But the change is still there. Having kids changes what I worry about. To me, the real issue of parenthood is that you constantly respond to other people's needs even when you don't feel like it.

Jan: That's right. That's what stretching is. At work or at church or out in the community you are a free agent. You *volunteer* to do things, or you make an agreement with your employer. And you are always free to move on.

Tony: If you can afford it...

Jan: But with kids, it's different. You just keep responding to their changing needs. It's like trying to hang on to a moving freight train. You go where it takes you.

Tony: For example, one time our son stopped making friends. So we took him to a therapist. That itself was a stretching experience because it caused us—me—to think about how we were communicating as a family. The idea came up that our son needed to shift from the mother-sponsored friends of a young boy to the father-sponsored friends of an adolescent.

Jan: He needed a stronger male bond.

Tony: Anyway, we decided on the civil air patrol. He didn't have to be a jock in the patrol, and there was a lot of structure, challenge and adventure. Someone had to take him to the meetings and support his interest until he could make friends and really get into it. And that someone was me. I didn't need another weekly meeting and something else to be responsible for. But I went anyway. And sure enough, after a while I joined the senior committee, ran the annual fund drive, got a uniform and became an assistant instructor.

Jan: C'mon, you didn't hate it that much. You really liked the flying.

Tony: True, but the point is that I got more than I bargained for. It was another stretching experience. It started as something *he* needed and ended up with something I became. I still go to some meetings—long after he's left the patrol.

145

Jan: That's happened a lot as our kids got older. We'd keep getting into new things. Now we joke about everything that's happened. We picture ourselves back in our old living room and we say, "Well, do you feel stretched enough?"

Tony: And the answer is "no." We've learned that stretching and growing is the meaning of life. I'm glad we decided to expand ourselves through parenthood. It's made me more than I ever expected to be. And I—we—plan to keep growing even though the kids are raised.

And so it goes through the stages of transformation that writers like Eric Erikson, George Vaillant and Gail Sheehy have mapped out. One becomes by turns: adult, citizen, lover, mate, parent, provider, contributor, leader, grandparent, sage, and survivor. For some they are just a series of experiences. For others they are a process of becoming an ever-greater self.$^\Omega$

Being Many Persons at Once

Although our capacity to appropriate many identities is large, most of us experience only one identity at a time. We exist as a single personality—like a balloon that expands but stays whole. But for some of us the limits of a single personality are too confining.

Joan is a schizophrenic. Her personality is split into several parts. She works in our office and does her job as well as anyone. But there is something strange about her conversation. She often speaks out of the blue, without

---

$^\Omega$ Or as Jung would have it, becoming is a meandering process of "individuation" in which each person takes on an individual combination of the great human Archetypes: hero, orphan, trickster, warrior, prince(ess), martyr, wanderer and magician. C.G. Jung, ed., *Man and His Symbols*, 1964, London, Aldus, passim. Carol S. Pearson, *The Hero Within*, 1986, NY, Harper Collins, passim.

reference to any previous conversation. She never calls me by name. She just begins by saying "oh."

One day she said to me, "Oh, I'm a schizophrenic. You know? Don't worry. I'm taking my medicine. Today I'm just Joan. But sometimes I'm Joan of Arc, you know, a very political person. Sometimes Joan Rivers, sort of wild and funny. Not really a saint at all. And sometimes I'm Joan Baez, a great singer. I don't really sing, but I like to write songs." Then she walked away.

Few of us are that extreme. But there is a value in being so free. How much more meaning could we cram into one lifetime if we could be psychologically as liberal as Joan?

All of Life's a Stage

Expanding the limits of personality is one of the services of literature, theater and movies. They put us in the skin of other persons. The better the work, the more absorbed I become in *being* this other person and sharing his or her meaning in life. Through literature I am a multitude of human possibilities.

Actors have a special privilege in this matter. They permit themselves to be more than one person at a time. They take on the mannerisms, the passions, the deeds and the very being of the characters they play. They absorb the new personality for the play. Sometimes they never lose it.

Antonio is a somewhat moody person when he's just being himself. But put him on stage and he comes alive. He lives in a small town. But not so small that they don't have community theater and shows for the kids. Sometimes he plays a gorilla. Sometimes an evil villain. Sometimes the worried father in the Miracle Worker. Sometimes Scrooge and sometimes Santa Claus.

"I am all of these," he says, "whenever I want to be."

Questions for Reflection

List all the roles you have played (or might play) in your life.

Do you ever take on the identity of a character in a book or movie? How long does the experience last?

What was your most stretching experience? Has the stretching ended?

Where do you keep all the people who you have become?

We are the river;
You are the sea.

Christian Hymn

COMMUNING WITH A LARGER REALITY

As we follow our path through the Realm of Being we come to a broad river that draws all lesser waters into its mighty flow. Clouds stirring over the distant mountains brew fresh drops to feed the torrent. Between the mountains and the river are fields and forests soaked with a sense of peaceful fluidity. The people who live here dip their spirits serenely in nature and breath the moist air of our common Being. These are the mystics who find meaning in communion. Their souls cannot be contained in their own being. They yearn for *unity* with a much larger being.

Merging with the Other

At the river's edge we see a boat landing where two Oriental men, Siddhartha and Vasudeva, ferry passengers on their raft. The river is the sacred Ganges. It's right to start here since we Westerners tend to believe that real mystics come from the East.

According to the story by Herman Hesse, Siddhartha experimented with many forms of meaning. He followed, one after another, the ways of the Brahmins, the ascetics, the scholars and the family patriarchs. But none of these satisfied his soul. At last he gave up seeking and became an ordinary boatman. One day while leaning on his oar, he heard voices in the river and wondered about their meaning. His friend, Vasudeva, encouraged him to listen further:

> The many-voiced song of the river echoed softly. Siddhartha looked into the river and saw many pictures in the flowing water. He saw his father, lonely, mourning for his son; he saw himself, lonely, also with the bonds of longing for his faraway son; he saw his son, also lonely, the boy eagerly advancing along the burning path of life's desires, each one concentrating on his goal, each one obsessed by his goal, each one suffering. The river's voice was sorrowful. It sang with yearning and sadness, flowing towards its goal.

> "Do you hear?" asked Vasudeva's mute glance. Siddhartha nodded. "Listen better!" whispered Vasudeva.

> Siddhartha tried to listen better. The picture of his father, his own picture, and the picture of his son all flowed into each other. [His wife] Kamala's picture also appeared and flowed on, and the picture of [his friend] Govinda and others emerged and passed on. They all became part of the river. It was the goal of all of them, yearning, desiring, suffering; and the river's voice was full of longing, full of smarting woe, full of insatiable desire. The river flowed on towards its goal. Siddhartha saw the river hasten, made up of himself and his relatives and all the people he had ever seen. All the waves and water hastened, suffering, towards goals, many goals, to the waterfall, to the sea, to the current, to the ocean and all goals were reached and each one was succeeded by another. The water changed to vapor and rose, became rain and came down again, became spring, brook and river, changed anew, flowed anew. But the yearning voice had altered. It still echoed sorrowfully, searchingly, but other voices accompanied it, voices of pleasure and sorrow, good and evil voices, laughing and lamenting voices, hundreds of voices, thousands of voices.

> Siddhartha listened. He was now listening intently, completely absorbed, quite empty, taking in everything. He

felt that he had now learned the art of listening. He had often heard all this before, all these numerous voices in the river, but today they sounded different. He could no longer distinguish the different voices—the merry voice from the weeping voice, the childish voice from the manly voice. They all belonged to each other: the lament of those who yearn, the laughter of the wise, the cry of indignation and groan of the dying. They were all interwoven and interlocked, entwined in a thousand ways. And all the voices, all the goals, all the yearnings, all the sorrows, all the pleasures, all the good and evil, all of them together was the world. All of them together was the stream of events, the music of life.

Herman Hesse, Siddhartha, *NY, New Directions, 1951, pp. 134ff. Abridged.*

At last he became one in being with them all.

The meaning of communion is that the mystic's being is not just his own. It breaks its natural boundaries to become one with your being—and mine—and indeed all being. This experience of unification is more dangerous than the expansion that occurs in knowledge or becoming. In these, you at least remain yourself. In communion, your being *merges with* the being of the other. You give up the control of your being and become swept up in a great river of being. You jump into the river and let yourself be carried along.$^{\Omega}$

Eastern mystics, like Siddhartha, emphasize a total and absolute merging of being. In the end we are all one. We are all the *same being* without difference, only seeming different. There is nothing left of me in the great river except a tiny wisp of consciousness—one little voice in the river's mighty roar.

$^{\Omega}$ Of course, the mystic stays in her own skin. The experience takes place through knowledge and spiritual affinity. Literally it is an act of knowledge, but the *intention*, the meaning, is to appreciate unity at a deeper level of being.

Brotherhood In the Vision Pit

Native people in the West hold another view of communion—not where being fuses together—but where people and nature live together like parts of a single organism. All are siblings in the Great Spirit, drawing nourishment from each other.

John Lame Deer, a medicine man of the South Dakota Sioux, was sixteen when he was taken to a narrow pit in the Black Hills and left alone for four days of meditation. He was to endure hunger, thirst and loneliness in hope of seeing a vision. The Spirit, he believed, was everywhere, and it would show itself through an animal, a bird, or some trees. Huddled in the vision pit, he smoked a peace pipe and sensed the closeness of all his ancestors. He wrapped himself in a quilt with a brightly colored star on it, which he called a star blanket. After a long wait sounds came to him in the darkness:

> —the cries of the wind, the whisper of the trees, the voices of nature, animal sounds, the hooting of an owl. Suddenly I felt an overwhelming presence. Down there with me in my cramped hole was a big bird. The pit was only as wide as myself, and I was a skinny boy, but that huge bird was flying around me as if he had the whole sky to himself. I could hear his cries, sometimes near and sometimes far, far away. I felt feathers or a wing touching my back and head. This feeling was so overwhelming that it was just too much for me. I trembled and my bones turned to ice. ... I took the sacred pipe in my hand and began to sing and pray: "Tunkashila, grandfather spirit, help me." But this did not help. I don't know what got into me, but I was no longer myself. I started to cry. Crying, even my voice was different. I sounded like an older man, I couldn't even recognize this strange voice. I used long-ago words in my prayer, words no longer used nowadays. I tried to wipe away my tears, but they couldn't

stop. In the end I just pulled that quilt over me, rolled myself up in it. Still I felt the bird wings touching me.

Slowly I perceived that a voice was trying to tell me something... "You are sacrificing yourself here to be a medicine man. In time you will be one. You will teach other medicine men. We are the fowl people, the winged ones, the eagles and the owls. We are a nation and you shall be our brother. You will never kill or harm any one of us. You are going to understand us whenever you come to seek a vision here on this hill..."

And again I heard the voice amid the bird sounds, the clicking of beaks, the squeaking and chirping. "You have love for all that has been placed on this earth, not like the love of a mother for her son, or a son for his mother, but a bigger love which encompasses the whole earth. You are just a human being, afraid, weeping under that blanket, but there is a great space within you to be filled with that love. All of nature can fit in there." I was shivering, pulling the blanket tighter around myself, but the voices repeated themselves over and over again, calling me "Brother, brother, brother." So this is how it is with me. Sometimes I feel like the first being in one of our Indian legends. This was a giant made of earth, water, the moon and the winds. He had timber instead of hair, a whole forest of trees. He had a huge lake in his stomach and a waterfall in his crotch. I feel like this giant. All of nature is in me, and a bit of myself is in all of nature.

J. Fire and R. Erdoes, Lame Deer, Seeker of Visions,
NY, Simon and Schuster, 1972, pp. 4f and 126.

Father Mountain and Mother Nature

Many things have changed since Lame Deer's experience of communion. The Black Hills are mostly civilized, and the roadsides bristle with garish billboards. But the hills are still there, and I thought I might recapture some of the old Sioux's vision.

In the heart of the hills is Black Elk Wilderness, topped by Harney Peak. I decided to climb its highest point, to be, as it were, with the father of mountains. I knew that I, along with a million other tourists, would violate once again the Treaty of 1868 which granted the Black Hills forever to the Sioux "as long as the sun shines and the grass grows." I apologized silently to Lame Deer and entered the wilderness as reverently as possible.

There was nothing I could do about the gaudy tourists, but I could carry up my drab old camping gear and stay overnight after they were gone. I promised to view the moon through the ponderosa and watch the eclipse expected that night. Perhaps, like the medicine man of old, I would have a vision.

I started from Sylvan Lake at noon under bright sunlight. The climb took only two and a half hours. I was surprised how easily my fifty year old legs accepted the load. This was a good sign. The path was wide and fairly gradual. Four teenage boys passed me on mountain bikes (though they were later turned back by a forest ranger). Three people rode by on horses. Several dozen hikers crossed on their way down. They carried plastic water jugs and wore tee shirts emblazoned with the names of colleges, baseball teams, designer labels and inane sayings (like "Truckers do it better", "Father's day off" or "Baby below"). I hefted my load to affirm its significance every time I passed these heathens.

The view from the top was panoramic. I could see a hundred miles into the prairie and look down on the lesser peaks and hills. I was looking down on the holy mountains, from God's point of view.

On the north side I saw thunderheads trailing sheets of rain as they swept to the east. Awesome! The spirits were showing their power on the distant peaks. I climbed away from the lookout tower to be alone. Hidden from view, I knelt on some grass and opened my arms to the heavens. Did they have anything to say to me?

"Boom," spoke a voice from above. "Boom, boom, boom." It was the voice of Father Mountain calling to Mother Nature in thunderous claps. I answered "Yes! Yes!" to these primal powers.

I felt bold enough to influence their movement. I was like a magician or rainmaker. I found a pine branch and made it into a worthy staff. I sawed away the twigs with my Swiss Army knife and ground off the remaining nubs against a boulder. The iron-age and stone-age combined. I pointed my staff at the darkest part of the thunderheads and by sustained force of will caused the writhing green and black mass to move and the lightening to fire.

Now comes the humbling part they usually don't tell you in books on mystical experience. In the late afternoon I regained my backpack just below the tree line and looked for a place to spend the night. I found some level spots with jutting rock platforms for viewing the moon but rejected them because they were too exposed to wind, lightning or runoff.

"Boom, boom!" The storm to the north was not sliding off as obediently as I had willed.

Finally, I chose a shelf under a shallow overhang. It was a partial cave so that half of my tent was under it and half in the open. The time was now six in the evening. The lightning strikes got closer and the booms louder. Mother Nature and Father Mountain were mating right over my head.

Fifteen feet from the tent was another indentation in the cliff wall. I huddled in it to cook my supper. Then the hail began—big gumball size hail. I dove into the tent and dragged all my belongings in after me. This was no family tent with lots of headroom. It was a backpacker's pup tent with space only to lay lengthwise. It was like being in a long tube, stuffed with gear and nowhere to move. So this was how I spent my night of meditation in my own kind of vision pit—prone and cramped and having terribly to go to the bathroom.

I suppose you already guessed that I never watched the moon, much less the lunar eclipse. Nor did I hear any bird voices. On the way down, however, I had an unexpected vision. It too was a vision of brotherhood. It started when I passed Cathedral Spires with their sharp needle points rising like Gothic towers in the crisp, blue sky. Rounding a break in the rocks I saw the profile of a human face on the last most spire. On top of another I saw a small boulder shaped like a human hand. People in the mountains, I thought. Father Mountain must love to feel his children close by if he has cradled them symbolically in his craggy folds. Thereafter, I greeted the gaudy, noisy tourists and their dogs and water bottles and tee shirts with more respect and humility. They were his children too. My modern brothers, wearing their own brand of brightly-colored star blankets.

Other Mystics of the West

Some of the most intense mystics I know are fishermen. They float all day on the water, totally absorbed in nature and the rituals of trolling, tackle and tactics. My Uncle Frank is such a mystic.

One day when I was twelve, Uncle Frank picked me up at 3:30 in the morning. I was so excited I hardly slept all night. There were just the two of us. I don't remember why my brother or Frank's own son didn't come along. The car was loaded with every possible provision: coffee, sandwiches, tackle, motor, the works. My uncle is an affable man, full of mischief and stories. So I knew this was going to be interesting. All the way up to the lake he talked incessantly. First it was about fishing: the kind of lures to use and how to hook the minnows just right—through the mouth, out the gill and back through the body at the tail. Then he talked about his own growing up. He told about letting the air out of tires and putting pennies on the trolley tracks. Fascinated, I pumped him for more information. So he told me about exploding firecrackers in the neighbors' garbage cans, the times he pulled the electric boom off the street car, and how his friend schemed to get some girls tipsy at a dance. This was macho stuff that my own dad never dared to tell me. I could tell that this was going to be a day of great masculine revelations.

But when the boat glided away from the dock my uncle turned into a different person. He became gravely quiet and totally absorbed in the business of fishing. I followed his mood and said nothing. We motored silently through a thick haze. I watched the sun's dull red orb rise stealthily above the trees like a giant wolf's eye bloodshot and hungry.

"There's the reef," he said. "We're going to troll for walleyes." That's about all he said the rest of the day. That and a few other directions. Two other things surprised me. One was the tiny one and a half horse motor he used. So small a motor for so macho a man! The other was how readily he let me drive it. Was it to let me have fun? Or was it so that he could devote all his attention to fixing the lures and testing the tension on the lines?

We fished all day, stopping only once to stretch our legs and eat lunch. This was way beyond my usual attention span. But the intense concentration of this man drew me into a meditative trance of my own. The throb of the motor, the thrum of the lines and the lapping of the shadowy-green waves all contributed to a dream-like state. The mood was broken only by five-minute spurts of excitement when we hooked a fish, played it and landed it. Even then, Uncle Frank never got too excited. He would net the creature into the boat, lay it on the bottom and stare at it for a while.

"Nice fish," he would say, "maybe a three pounder." Then he would stroke its glossy side to calm it and put it carefully on the stringer.

On the way home he started talking again, as if he came out of a reverie. He revealed family history I never dreamed to be true. Why, for example, Grandpa had a different last name from the rest of his brothers and sisters. Uncle Frank was back to his regular, impish self. But out on the water he was mystic, as if his soul had surged over the side of the boat and merged with the elements of sun and sky, spoon and sinker.

Other such mystics are gardeners, mechanics, artists, weavers, musicians and craftsmen—all who experience a deep unity between themselves and their natural materials.

A Green-Eyed Urban Mystic

One day I was sitting by a quiet lake in a small town enjoying the late summer sunshine when I met a man on vacation from Illinois. We talked for a while about baseball teams and the beauty of the day. I pointed out the Indian burial mounds at the far end of the park. He seemed to know something about Indian customs and folklore. I commented on how much we have changed the land and made it harder to commune with nature, even in this lovely spot. This is what he said:

"Some people think I'm crazy and maybe you will too. But I love the modern world we live in. We all love it, of course, because the things we manufacture make us more comfortable and efficient. But I don't just love the comfort. I love the artificial world because it seems natural—the way the world was to the Indians. The people who think I'm crazy are the pure nature lovers. They say, let's get back to nature where we flow with the wind and soak in the rain.

"Personally, I like to be close to cities. Whenever I drive into Chicago after miles and miles of cornfields, I feel a special excitement. I feel part of this gigantic construction. I zoom down its canyons and flow along in its rivers of people. Sure, it's dirty. But so is nature. I like to breathe in its smells: French fry exhaust from greasy diners, popcorn from theaters, ammonia from window-cleaning buckets, that electric odor from subways, and diesel fumes from buses. You see why people think I'm crazy? But I love it. It's the aroma of life. The Indians talk about grabbing smoke from the peace pipe and rubbing it all over themselves. Well, that's how I feel about the smell of new tires or bindery glue. I want to grab it and smear it all over me.

"I work on the 21st floor of a skyscraper. Lots of glass, stainless steel, fluorescent light, trendy carpet and freshly painted walls. The closest thing to nature is a bed of philodendron in the lobby and the fish tank in the boss's office. My own work-space is a formica counter built into a cubicle of beige upholstered panels. There's some cream colored file cabinets and a plastic lamp with a rust-colored shade. No mahogany desk for me. Yet I love this place. Every day when I come in I say, 'Hi lamp, hi formica, hi cabinets and papers and clipboard.' These are my work buddies, my artificial brothers.

"Right in the middle of the desk is my computer. It takes me to another plane of consciousness. Once I get it booted up and humming, I get lost in it. It's an endless mystery of letters, lines and numbers that I communicate with. On the one hand, I can shape it any way I want. And on the other hand, I have to respect its logic, structure and limitations. I once read a passage by John Paul Sartre that described a skier making tracks in new fallen snow. The guy was the first person on the slope, free to create any marks he wanted as long as he tended downhill. That's how I feel with my computer. I plunge into its soft green space. I can put anything on the screen I want as long as I follow the "slope" of the program and the aims of our business.

"Some people are afraid of the computer. They think it gives off rays that sterilize or blind them. I find the rays are warm and energizing. They sink into my brain and turn it on.

"The computer has taught me something else about myself. I used to think that all my intelligence was in my head, as if I first had thoughts and then expressed them in writing. But I find that I think better with my fingers on the keyboard, as if a large part of my intelligence is really in my hands. Maybe artists and pianists feel the same communion with their instruments and materials. So a big part of my consciousness is tactile and bound up with this thinking machine. It's an extension of my self. I'm glad to come into my artificial world every day and plug into its vast expanse of being. I put my mark on it, and when I leave at night the glow stays with me for several hours. I have to drum my fingers in order to think. Am I crazy or what?"

After he left, I thought maybe he revealed a truth I had not realized before. That communion with being is not limited to nature. A real mystic sees unity everywhere.

Holy Communion

Do you remember Grace whom I introduced in the first chapter? She sat quietly through many conversations with Dave and Susan and the others in our group. But when we got to this topic she suddenly crossed and uncrossed her legs, signaling that she had something to say. We all looked at her and waited. "I'm not much of an outdoors person," she said. "Nor do I think much about communion with nature. I'm certainly not mesmerized by computers, but I do like the idea of our souls being somehow joined in God."

She hesitated for a moment, but feeling our gaze, plunged on. "I'm really more of a church person. I love to sit alone in a big church and watch the lights sparkle in the stained glass windows, as if the stories of the saints there blended with our stories. It's even better when someone is practicing a Bach prelude on the organ. I hear everyone praising God in one thunderous voice.

"I like the service too, when people press against me in the pew. Though packed together, everyone is friendly. We join hands and sing together. There's a special odor in the air too— a mixture of mustiness, furniture polish, incense, and freshly washed clothes. It makes me think that God is smiling down on us, happy that we are all members of the same body, God's body.

"I like to imagine that this same coming together is happening all over the world. As the sun circles the globe on Sunday morning, it brings the hour of service to each part of the world. One by one the people of the world awake to join in a common experience of being brothers and sisters in the Lord."

Questions for Reflection

What is your favorite place in nature? What do you enjoy about being there?

How deeply do you feel the joys and sorrows of others? Are they the same as yours?

Do you get absorbed in your work and hobbies? What (perhaps) are you communing with?

If your church celebrates a communion service, how do you feel as it finishes?

They also serve
who only stand
and wait.

Milton

ENTERING THE GREAT BEYOND

We are approaching the end of our journey through the realms of Having, Doing and Being. At every step the land has yielded a wealth of meaning. Lately however, the terrain has become thinner and less populated. And now we find ourselves at the very edge of Being. What lies before us is an empty wilderness from which no traveler has ever returned. There is no path to follow, nor any landmark by which to take our bearings. We are aware only of an immense distance and a howling wind that beckons us to a meaning utterly beyond us. Should we take this last step to what is called "transcendence"?

Finding It in the Desert

The desert is a favorite place for seekers of transcendence—hermits, the desert fathers and other holy people. I tried it myself a few times in the southwest United States. But I kept running into settlements, power lines and beer cans.

Once, however, in Israel I had a chance to go into the real desert, the desert of the ancient prophets and anchorites. I took a bus to a kibbutz not far from the ruins of Jericho. I swam in the Dead Sea, and sure enough, I floated like a cork.

Then, as dusk approached, I hiked about a mile into the open desert until I could no longer observe the Dead Sea—or anything else. Just the endless spread of sand. At first it seemed humorous. I thought of Shelley's poem about the proud, sneering king whose statue was found half sunk in "the lone and level sands." I stood on my knapsack, since there was no other pedestal, and pretended to be this king. I shouted:

> "My name is Ozymandias, King of Kings:
> Look on my works, ye mighty, and despair!"

No one laughed. No sound came back at all. This land without features returned no echo or response. It was so quiet I heard my ears ring and my heart pound.

Is this what the Great Beyond is like? I wondered. To be so intensely *aware*, with nothing to be aware of?

I felt a little better when the stars came out. Friendly dots of something familiar. Of just something! But soon they filled the dry clear sky and surrounded me like a swarm of lightning bugs. All of space was the same—enormous and without shape. It began to swirl and I started to get dizzy. I had to sit down and close my eyes not to be overcome by the sameness and nothingness of it all.

I spent the night huddled in my sleeping bag. I slept poorly and prayed a lot. I didn't go into the desert to pray. Prayer just happens when you realize that the ultimate meaning of life knocks you completely off your pedestal.

Diminishment

Several years ago my in-laws retired to a beautiful resort area in Arkansas. My family drove from Minneapolis to Chicago to wish them farewell. We got two boxes of things they wouldn't be using any more—mostly memorabilia from my wife's high school days. We drove back with the stuff tied to the top of our car.

Two years later they returned to Chicago because they missed their old community. We got another two boxes—this time mostly fishing tackle. Within two years John suffered a stroke. He recovered but felt cold all the time and couldn't walk in the snow. So they moved to a mobile home in Tampa where some old friends lived. This time we got five boxes of tools and garden implements because their retirement community provided all the outdoor services.

During the next year John was hospitalized several times for diabetes. He seldom left the house. Mae was diagnosed with Alzheimer's. My wife started to manage their affairs, and their old friend took over the checkbook. After a while Mae and John no longer ate regular meals. Food spoiled in the refrigerator. We couldn't keep flying back and forth to Florida. They had to be where we could care for them. We found a residence for them in Minnesota. It was a nice two-room apartment with a lovely view. All their meals would be provided, as well as medical attention.

They moved in August, after selling their prized furniture and appliances. My son and I drove the rest of their possessions up in a rented truck. Our load included all of John's underwear as well as his insulin which he "forgot" to take on the airplane. Maureen had to buy her dad some underwear and re-fill his prescription. They were waiting anxiously when we pulled in. Not everything in the truck fit in their two rooms. So we stored some items and gave others away. Ten boxes came to our house—mostly dishes and room decorations. We were starting to have two sets of everything: towel racks, cleansers, sink mats and book ends.

After Thanksgiving John had another diabetes attack and moved to a nursing home. Mae's memory became so bad that she couldn't stay alone. We installed her in a medium care room in another wing of the residence. Over the Christmas holidays we again filled and carried boxes because we had to empty their apartment. Fifteen boxes came to our house. By this time we had a TV set for every member of the family. It wasn't the Christmas we wanted.

John died in February. The day after the funeral was the last time that Mae expressed awareness of time. "When does the funeral start?" she asked while dressing at her brother-in-law's house in Chicago.

"The funeral was yesterday," we answered, adding details about the friends she had mourned with.

"Oh, isn't it awful," she said. "to be cheated of these memories." Thereafter she lived only in the present. And the present came in shorter and shorter spurts.

In April we moved her to a full-scale nursing home. This time *all* the boxes came to our house—including the religious medals, John's old police badge and the jewelry that Mae could no longer remember where she put.

Part of life is diminishment. There comes a change in being that we do not choose, until, as the poet Fredrico Garcia Lorca, says:

> Now I am no longer I;
> Nor is my house my own to sell.

Life is a Pilgrimage

Some people say that life is a pilgrimage—a journey from birth to death. Pilgrims do not collect souvenirs. Rather their baggage becomes lighter as they travel and their companions go only part of the way. Their strength is the very nakedness that allows them to move easily across the borders of being.

I was present at my son's birth. Dressed in a green hospital gown, I held my wife's hand as she went into the operating room. I was never so excited in my life. It was a Cesarean. With a spinal block there would be no pain, so everyone, including the "patient," was in an eager mood. Even the doctors were upbeat and chatted pleasantly between their serious duties. I tried to focus on my wife, to smile and look in her eyes. But I couldn't help glancing over the low partition at her waist to see what the doctors were doing with the great mound of life beneath their scalpel.

"Well, look here," one doctor said at last, "a solid little guy." Then suddenly out of the folds of surgical sheets he appeared. My son! How small. Completely naked and skinny. Just a tiny bit of life sprung, as it were, out of nothing.

Of course, he has grown up and is now a vigorous young man. But I remember that first appearance before he took his first breath. When he was as small as a human being can be, having only the attribute of being. I remember his eyes, hardly open and staring at me, as if to say, "What are you doing here?"

A contrasting image is the only death I actually attended. It was a woman approximately sixty years old, suffering from cancer. I didn't know her personally, and I don't remember her name. I went along with two friends who wanted to visit her. They thought I would add the care of the larger community. I tried my best to perform this duty, but I was not able to give much. On the contrary, she gave me more by suffering my presence.

Her body had slowly wasted from the cancer. She was so tiny and thin, barely raising a lump under the hospice sheets. One friend held her hand and stroked her cheek. The other companion said, "We're praying for you. We love you so much." I stammered something about having a meaningful life. The chaplain came in and said she could hope for new life in the resurrection.

She didn't respond to any of these words. I don't know what she was thinking, poised there at the edge of being. I don't know what meaning she found in life, or what thoughts she had if any. I just remember as she took her last breath, she stared at me. Her eyes seemed only to say, "What are you doing here?"

Something Beyond All That

"All that I have written is so much dross." I suppose I could make that statement about this book. Actually it was Thomas Aquinas who said it. After writing many works, including three tomes summarizing wisdom up to his time, he knew there was a further meaning he couldn't put into words.

This ultimate meaning is elusive and slippery. Each experience contains something of it. Yet, looking back on many experiences, he knew that life is not just the sum of our experiences. In a way, they simply define what it is not.

One of his most poignant chapters asks what is the ultimate good that human beings seek. He discards the candidates one by one because of their limitation:

- Not possessions
- Not pleasure

- Not fame
- Not good works

In the end, he concludes, the only unlimited good is God. And therefore the ultimate meaning of life must be the contemplation of God. He quotes St. Augustine, "Our hearts are restless until they rest in thee."

So what then is God? Aquinas answers that question in the same way. In this life we know God only negatively, by what God is not:

- Not matter
- Not life
- Not person
- Not time
- Not spirit
- Not being

God, he concludes, is beyond all that, without any limit or distinction. The fullness of God *and* the meaning of life are utterly beyond. Then, at the end of his days, looking back on what he had written so eloquently, Thomas says, "It's not that either."

The final meaning of life transcends all our small human meanings. We can only let go and trust that an ultimate meaning is there, at the source and end of all being.

Questions for Reflection

What losses have you suffered? What did you learn from these experiences?

If you lost all your possessions, your companions and your strength, what would you have left?

What do you think lies beyond death? How do you feel about it—ready, excited, awed, scared?

CONCLUSION

We return now from our journey through the realms of Having, Doing and Being, back to your living room or den, so you can claim the meaning of your own life.

Whoever you are,
claim your own
at any hazard!

Walt Whitman

CONCLUSION

How to Claim Your Meaning

Let's start by asking what we got out of the journey. For myself, I learned a lot and I feel grateful. Remember the yellow brick road? Well, we've arrived in Oz. Hopefully, the characters who traveled with us have found their brains, their future and their heart. As for me, the cowardly lion, I have found my courage and said what I believe more clearly than ever before. A line in the Talmud says:

> Three things a man should do before he dies:
> Have a child, plant a tree and write a book.

I planted a sugar maple when my son was born and a fir tree at my daughter's birth. So now I've done all three, and I'm glad.

Is This Worthwhile for You?

But what have *you* taken from this work? You haven't said much throughout the reading. I noticed that you skipped some of the reflections. I understand that; I do the same when I read other people's books. But how do you feel about where we have been?

Perhaps you feel satisfied. The journey was interesting; you learned something; but now you are ready for something else. If so, I wish you well.

On the other hand, you may feel some discontent or puzzlement because you have not yet found your own meaning on the journey. Perhaps, like my friends Dave, Susan and Grace, you still feel:

- A little shallow sometimes
- Not altogether sure what your life will add up to
- Not able to put a name on all that you have experienced.

Or maybe you are wondering why you are attracted to forms of meaning that your friends don't care about. How can you enjoy rather than fight over these differences?

If you have questions or feelings like these, then I invite you to reflect further on your personal philosophy using the suggestions and exercises that follow. Or if you are just curious, read on, perhaps for ideas about helping others.

Some Ideas and Suggestions

I can only give you suggestions, since there are no rules of personal philosophy. As Victor Frankl says, choosing your inmost attitude is the one thing in which you are most free. It's hard to have rules and be free. It's also hard to have rules about choices that are so abundant. As we have seen, there are numerous meanings to choose from. It's also hard to have rules about things that change. Even our very self—our being—keeps expanding and moving on.

And yet there are some practical steps we can take—not to pin our meaning down like a dead butterfly—but to entrust enough meaning into words so that we can call it our own in spite of its ever-unfolding nature.

Let me offer some guidelines for your consideration. Then we will do some exercises to put the guidelines into practice.

1. Focus on What Attracts You

First, focus on a source of meaning that attracts you. As Joseph Campbell says, the best advice is "to follow your bliss." If you didn't recognize your bliss in the meanings we explored on this journey, create your own. Our fifteen examples are but a few of the most common. They are only a good place to start.

The biggest obstacle to choosing what attracts you is fear of making a mistake—fear that you are not choosing the "best" or the "right" meaning. I think this fear is unfounded as long as you remember the criteria we set out at the beginning. If what you choose is intensely personal, takes you out of yourself, makes sense, gives purpose to living, and is honorable, there is little to fear.

You may be wondering, nevertheless, if there is some implied "better" or "worse" even in the meanings we have defined. Being a clever person, you don't want to choose some meaning that will later draw ridicule. I can only tell you that there is nobility in all the types of meaning we have explored. True, the professional philosophers extol the realm of Being in their books. But that is their job—to illuminate this less visible realm so the rest of us can appreciate it. Away from their desks, they too are lovers, parents, collectors, and adventurers. They too have personal lives in the realms of Having and Doing as well as Being. The truth is that each human being lives in all three domains. Each is valuable. And blissful meaning is found equally in all three.

2. Choose What Fits You—Not Someone Else

The second guideline supports the first: choose what fits you, not someone else. We can sometimes be misled by what people around us think. That was Dave's problem. He thought he was shallow because he felt no personal connection to the things his wife found meaningful. After thinking about it, he found that his own meaning was just different, not less than hers. The truth is that there are many forms of meaning, and individuals *prefer* one form over another. Seeing the variety of valid meanings helps us to embrace one that is right for us.

It helps to see that these preferences are natural and not due merely to whim. I see a partial explanation for these differences in the theory of personality type.

Psychologists tell us we are born with individual tendencies. Some of us are introverts and others extroverts. Some are intuitive, some sense-oriented, some feeling-oriented, and so forth. Let's assume this is true.

We can then see that different persons are drawn to meanings that fit their type. For example, introverts may prefer the more intellectual forms of meaning such as knowledge and transcendence. Whereas extroverts may be more likely to prefer adventure, achievement and contribution. Persons more oriented to logical thinking may prefer a meaning that stresses order, while those who are more oriented to feeling, poetry and sentiment are likely to prefer love, tradition or mystical unity.

I don't believe there is anything necessary about this distribution. Anybody can adopt any form of meaning. But it helps to explain why we don't agree on the *one* meaning of life. It's just natural to prefer the themes that fit our style.

There are many schemes to describe personality styles— from the "temperaments" of the ancients to the popular Myers-Briggs scales of today. One easy-to-use explanation is the concept of "social style." It was invented by David Merrill and elaborated by several researchers, including my colleagues at Wilson Learning Corporation.

Social style sorts people into types based on how they behave in social situations. Some people tend to behave more assertively than others. They characteristically make a greater effort to influence the opinions and actions of others. Thus all people can be arranged along a scale of assertiveness—some are more tell-assertive and some are more ask-assertive. A second scale measures people's responsiveness—how much they tend to show their emotions in social situations. Task-directed individuals behave in a cool and controlled manner, and people-directed individuals behave in a spontaneous and outgoing manner.

The two scales placed at right angles create a matrix:

Task-Directed

Analytical Style	Driving Style
Amiable Style	Expressive Style

Ask Assertive   Tell Assertive

People-Directed

© 1989, Wilson Learning Corporation.
Used with permission.

The matrix defines four "social styles":

1. The driving style tends to act in a controlled and assertive manner. People of this style focus on making serious events happen in the world around them in a straightforward, businesslike manner.

2. The expressive style tends to act in an equally assertive but more spontaneous and affable way. People of this

style focus on making human events more dramatic and good humored.

3.   The amiable style tends to act in a less assertive way. They are more likely to ask a question than to tell an opinion. Yet they are warm and spontaneous. People of this style influence others by listening, affirmation and quiet conversation.

4.   The analytical style also tends to ask rather than to tell, but in a more task-oriented way. People of this style focus on gathering facts, making precise judgments, and urging full consideration of the issues when making decisions.

Every human being can find a comfortable place in this matrix—a "comfort zone." Our comfort zone is where we most often behave, not withstanding our ability to behave more or less assertively or responsively as occasions demand.

This schema explains many differences between human beings. For example, it explains why it's sometimes hard for people of opposite styles to communicate well. It explains why some people prefer certain professions—the analytical accountant versus the expressive entertainer. People often arrange their occupations, their spousal choices and their social life to fit (or complement) the tendencies of their style.

The same factors can influence the type of meaning that a person prefers. Some of the themes we explored in earlier chapters may appeal more to one style than to another.

Here is a way to look at it:

Analytical Style	Driving Style
• Order • Knowledge	• Achievement • Contribution
Amiable Style	**Expressive Style**
• Love • Communion	• Adventure • Becoming

Not all the themes we covered fit in this matrix because some are unrelated to style—such as property and salvation. Yet some *are* related, and this relationship can shed light on our preferences.

It should not surprise you, for example, if you are a driver, that you find more meaning in task or business achievements than you do in loving relationships or mystical communion. The former is just more natural to your style. There is nothing wrong with you to have this preference. One-fourth of the population is with you. At the same time there is no law of social style that says you can't or shouldn't pursue other forms of meaning. They are just likely to be somewhat harder for you and not readily as satisfying.

Did you notice the social styles of my three friends? Dave was a driver, interested in achievement. Susan was an irrepressible expressive, bubbling with enthusiasm for many possibilities in the future. Grace was an amiable, attracted by love of family and a sense of communion. And finally, yours truly, representing the only remaining style, tried mightily to explain life's meaning in a logical, systematic way.

You can use social style to help decide which form(s) of meaning is most appropriate for you. Ask yourself these questions:

- Am I more or less assertive than most people?

- Am I more or less responsive than most people?

Ask your friends what they think. If from that information you make up your mind about your social style, then you can see from the chart above which theme(s) of meaning may be more likely to satisfy you.

Equally important, you can see which ones (usually those in the opposite corner of the diagram) you are likely to find the *least* appealing. This can be a sound basis for your choosing not to pursue them. It can also help you understand why you can't agree with certain friends about the meaning of life. What they care about may be right for their style but not for yours.

3. Focus on Two or Three Themes

The third guideline for choosing your meaning is to concentrate on a small number of themes that are most important to you. It is likely that one alone is not enough. Total single-mindedness is boring, both to ourselves and to others (remember Jody's grandfather). And fifteen is too many to be really personal and intense. As a rule, most human beings can hold about three to five things in their mind at the same time. So if you want a practical way to grasp and articulate your philosophy of life, you should focus on a small number of themes and let the rest take care of themselves.

My recommendation is to look for one form of meaning in each of the three great Realms. Like a well-balanced meal, a diet of meaning that includes something from each domain is probably the most satisfying and healthy.

4. Appreciate All Meanings

At the same time, it is worthwhile to reflect on and appreciate all forms of meaning. I say "appreciate," but not "concentrate on." I hope that appreciation has been a benefit you derived from reading this book—that you have seen a wide spectrum of possibilities and that each one has found some resonance in your soul. I hope the ones you found least interesting were not just discarded like so many pieces of junk mail that told you what you don't want. At least they could give you some empathy for other people—especially those you live with. While working on this book, for example, I have gained a much deeper appreciation of the meaning my son gets from automobiles. To me they are just a means of transportation. But to him they are real treasures. This realization gives me a clue about how to share meaning with him.

But more than empathy, I hope you found some personal value in each theme we looked at. Our total capacity for meaning is greater than the few things we can concentrate on. All our thoughts and experiences accumulate into our total personality. All the things we find meaningful—the big and the small, the named and the unnamed—settle in our soul. The psychologist Thomas Moore expresses the guideline this way:

> Here we come upon an important rule, applicable to religious spirituality and to stories, dreams, and pictures of all kinds. The intellect wants a summary of meaning—all well and good for the purposeful nature of the mind. But the soul craves depth of reflection, many layers of meaning, nuances without end, references and allusions and pre-figurations. All these enrich the texture of an image or story and please the soul by giving it much food for rumination.
>
> Thomas Moore, Care of the Soul,
> NY, Harper Collins, 1992, p. 235

I hope that the many meanings we have explored have added something to that depth of reflection for you. Said another way, we do not have to reject other meanings in order to cherish our favorite.

5. Declare What You Stand For

Notwithstanding the value in all forms of meaning, it is still important to focus on the few themes that are most important to you. That's because meaning as we have treated it *is* a matter of intellect, will and purpose. It is not just an accumulation of experiences that we carry along behind us. It is something we project forward, the reason we get up in the morning, the thing we stand for. Life is like a tapestry woven from many strands. But only a few master threads run from end to end and give cohesion to the whole.

Therefore, the last guideline is to make some declaration, some *commitment*, about the meaning of your life. Forcing yourself to choose one or more master threads will give you a greater sense of authorship in this slippery business of leading a meaningful life. There is, of course, more to human wisdom than we can put in words, but if we can't name its most important parts and act on their behalf, how can we call it wisdom?

That's why in the exercises ahead I will ask you to stand up, clear your throat and declare yourself for some meaning.

And don't worry if it changes over time. Why should it not change in a creature whose very being expands and transcends? A declaration of meaning is not a vow forever. It is a statement about what you find most meaningful now. As Carlos Castaneda says, "Any path is only a path. There is no affront to yourself or others in dropping it if that is what your heart tells you to do." Meaning is dynamic and expansive, just as your being is. Even what you drop will still be part of you. You can't get rid of a real meaning. It settles in your soul, as Moore suggests. The only tragedy, in my view, is to die before you awaken to any meaning. The more meaning you can manage in your whole lifetime, the better. But in order to manage any of it you have to name at least some of it.

Some Exercises to Determine Your Preferences

The rest of this chapter is a series of exercises that you can do in private or with others to reflect on which theme(s) holds the most meaning for you.

Note:

To order a workbook with exercises to use with a group, visit: **WhyGetUpInTheMorning.com**

REVIEW EXERCISE

The first exercise is to review the meanings we have explored and note what your reactions have been.

1. Review the summary chart on the next page.

2. Leaf back through the book and read what you underlined or wrote at the end of each chapter.

3. Note the ideas that most appeal to you on the lines below.

4. If you wish, share your ideas with someone else. Write down their comments.

_____

_____

_____

_____

_____

Ways of Finding Meaning in Life

Realms	Themes	Variations and Hints	
Having *Close relation-ships with people and Things*	Having someone to love	To care for someone special To be part of a vibrant family To watch my kids grow up	**Being Saved** *An acute awareness of being dependent in any or all 3 realms*
	Being cared about	To know that someone loves me To know that God cares about me To be noticed by important people	
	Enjoying beauty and treasure	To let things express who I am To collect interesting or beautiful things To exchange gifts	
	Getting a fair share	To have a full life To have a fair share of good things To know there is justice in the world	
	Having a sense of order	To have everything clean and in place To feel the pride of good craftsmanship To live by a well thought-out plan	
Doing *Creating meaning through purpose-ful action*	Achieving a great goal	To make something of value To take on and finish big projects To keep promises I have made	
	Making a contribution	To make the world a better place To do the little extra that people like To act out my part in history	
	Going on a great adventure	To see life as a great journey To see life as one or two great events To be involved in the drama of life	
	Following honored traditions	To do what our forefathers did To follow the rituals of the seasons To re-live the life of the Lord	
	Doing the right thing	To live as honorably as others To live by a higher law To do the right thing at any cost	
Being *Appreci-ating the deeper forces of Nature and Spirit*	Being present in the world	To be excited about being with people To appreciate the wonder of being To feel at peace for just existing	
	Knowing and sharing the truth	To know a lot about a special subject To teach or explain things to others To see the connection of all things	
	Becoming an ever-greater self	To make self-changing commitments To grow and stretch in many ways To be many people in oneself	
	Being in communion with others	To feel one with Nature or God To get absorbed in hobbies or activities To call all beings brothers and sisters	
	Entering the great beyond	To let-go To live simply To accept whatever comes	

185

REFLECTIVE QUESTIONNAIRE

This questionnaire will help you review the themes of meaning in a systematic way. It is not a scientific questionnaire but a structured series of questions to guide your reflection.

Instructions:

1. Turn to the "Reflective Questionnaire" on the next page. As you read each question, think of an event in your life that relates to the question.

2. Circle a number on the scale from 1 to 5 for each question. A "1" means this idea is not true or attractive to you; a "5" says it is very true or attractive to you.

3. Write down any thoughts or personal examples in the column labeled "Examples."

4. After you have finished the entire questionnaire, look back to see if there is a pattern in the numbers.

5. If you have high scores in all or most of the questions associated with one theme, then that type of meaning is probably important to you.

6. Spend more time in those areas where your scores are high to write down further examples and reflections.

7. Write down (in Part Two of the questionnaire) what this means for you, and what personal philosophy you draw from it.

REFLECTIVE QUESTIONNAIRE

Theme/Questions	How True for me	Examples
Having Someone to Love		
To share myself with people	1-2-3-4-5	
To care for someone special	1-2-3-4-5	
To be part of a vibrant family	1-2-3-4-5	
To watch my kids grow and succeed.	1-2-3-4-5	
Being Cared About		
To know someone loves me	1-2-3-4-5	
To know I have been chosen	1-2-3-4-5	
To know that God cares about me	1-2-3-4-5	
To be noticed by important people	1-2-3-4-5	
Enjoying Beauty and Treasure		
To have nice things	1-2-3-4-5	
To let things express who I am	1-2-3-4-5	
To collect interesting or beautiful things	1-2-3-4-5	
To exchange gifts with friends	1-2-3-4-5	
Getting a Fair Share		
To have a full life	1-2-3-4-5	
To have a fair share of good things	1-2-3-4-5	
To know there is justice in the world	1-2-3-4-5	
To get what I deserve	1-2-3-4-5	
Having a Sense of Order		
To make things as right as possible	1-2-3-4-5	
To have everything clean and in place	1-2-3-4-5	
To feel the pride of good craftsmanship	1-2-3-4-5	
To live by a well thought-out plan	1-2-3-4-5	

Theme/Questions	How True for me	Examples
Achieving a Great Goal		
To make something of value	1-2-3-4-5	
To take on big projects and finish them	1-2-3-4-5	
To keep promises I have made	1-2-3-4-5	
To use my talents to the fullest	1-2-3-4-5	
Making a Contribution		
To make the world a better place	1-2-3-4-5	
To make a difference by my work	1-2-3-4-5	
To care that the job is done right	1-2-3-4-5	
To play my part in history or evolution	1-2-3-4-5	
Going on a Great Adventure		
To see life as a great journey	1-2-3-4-5	
To have participated in a great event	1-2-3-4-5	
To be part of the action again and again	1-2-3-4-5	
To get power from a youthful adventure	1-2-3-4-5	
Following Honored Traditions		
To do what people have always done	1-2-3-4-5	
To do what great heroes have done	1-2-3-4-5	
To follow the footsteps of our forefathers	1-2-3-4-5	
To re-live the life of the Lord	1-2-3-4-5	
Doing the Right Thing		
To do the right thing at all times	1-2-3-4-5	
To be a person of honor and integrity	1-2-3-4-5	
To follow the dictates of conscience	1-2-3-4-5	
To live by God's law	1-2-3-4-5	

Theme/Questions	How True for me	Examples
Finding Salvation		
To know my weaknesses are forgiven	1-2-3-4-5	
To be spared of evil or addiction	1-2-3-4-5	
To feel Okay—one day at a time	1-2-3-4-5	
To know my prayers are answered	1-2-3-4-5	
Being Present in the World		
To be excited about being with people	1-2-3-4-5	
To appreciate the wonder of being	1-2-3-4-5	
To feel amazed by my human powers	1-2-3-4-5	
To feel at peace for just existing	1-2-3-4-5	
Knowing and Sharing the Truth		
To know a lot about a special subject	1-2-3-4-5	
To understand the reasons for things	1-2-3-4-5	
To teach or explain things to others	1-2-3-4-5	
To preserve some truth for the future	1-2-3-4-5	
Becoming a Greater Self		
To play many roles in life	1-2-3-4-5	
To savor every phase of life	1-2-3-4-5	
To grow and stretch in many ways	1-2-3-4-5	
To carry many people in myself	1-2-3-4-5	
Being in Communion		
To feel close to Nature or God	1-2-3-4-5	
To be one with all people—all being	1-2-3-4-5	
To get absorbed in hobbies or activities	1-2-3-4-5	
To call all beings brother and sister	1-2-3-4-5	

Theme/Questions	How True for me	Examples
Entering the Great Beyond		
To let-go of all that I have	1-2-3-4-5	
To accept whatever comes in life	1-2-3-4-5	
To yearn for life beyond death	1-2-3-4-5	
To trust that meaning is in God's hands	1-2-3-4-5	

Part Two

What conclusions do you draw from your answers? What do they say about your personal philosophy?

_____

_____

_____

_____

_____

_____

MOST SIGNIFICANT EVENTS

Sometimes it helps to go from experience to interpretation. This exercise helps you interpret your personal experiences.

1. Quickly jot down important events that occurred in your life. List them in the left-hand column. Don't think about them. Just write down a word or two to remind you of the event.

2. Now review the list more slowly. In the right-hand column write down what was meaningful about each event.

3. Compare what you have written to the themes described in this book. Have you perhaps found a meaning we have not considered?

Some important events of my life have been:	Each is meaningful because:

HOPES FOR THE FUTURE

The key to meaning is often hidden in our hopes. Think about what you want to have, do or be before you die. Review the list for clues to your personal philosophy.

Answer the following questions

1. Before I die, I would really like to have:

2. Something I'd really like to do before I die is:

3. No matter what happens, I want to be:

THE GREAT CELEBRATION

Imagine a great celebration is being given in your honor. One hundred people are talking about why your life has been so important. Five friends come to the microphone to summarize the meaning and value of your life. Who are they? What would they say?

1. _____

_____

_____

2. _____

_____

_____

3. _____

_____

_____

4. _____

_____

_____

5. _____

_____

_____

THE EPITAPH

Our lives are too rich to sum up in just a few words. But in the end, one or two things will be *most* important. And some few words have to go on our headstone.

What would you prefer to have said about you:

Here Lies

_____

About this person, know ye that:

_____

_____

_____

_____

_____

EPILOGUE

A Final Resting Place

I started this book in one cemetery, so I might as well end it in another.

Up the hill from Plymouth Rock is a burial ground of the early settlers of my country. At the top of the hill in the shade of many gnarled and ancient trees stands an obelisk marking the original burial site of Governor William Bradford. Nearby are the graves of other builders of the new world. People like Thomas Cooper and "ye wife Hannah."

The sense of meaning is great in this quiet place where their journey ended. Sitting on the bench near the obelisk and looking out over the ocean, I realized how much meaning these remarkable people experienced. They performed great deeds, like crossing the sea and founding a country. They sacrificed the treasures of one world and gained those of another. They loved their families and founded an ever-expanding community. They broke some traditions but started others. Theirs was a great adventure. They lived honorably. They preserved knowledge and passed it on. They prayed to be one with their God and all the saints.

Bury me there—with William Bradford and Thomas and Hannah Cooper. I think I could rest in peace in such a place.

And what epitaph would I like?

Well, I am, of course, embarrassed to publish it here. Just as you are probably embarrassed to share your inscription from the previous exercise. After all, it is customary to let other people write our epitaph—the one we *deserve* rather than the one we prefer.

And yet the whole point of this book is to help everyone, including myself, to claim some preferred meaning and to refuse to leave the final words to the confusion of bereaved relatives or the guesswork of unknowing undertakers. We need, at least, to give them some guidance if not the ultimate judgment.

So, in that spirit, I will be pleased if my friends choose to write something like "practical philosopher" on my stone. If this book succeeds in its purpose, I further hope they might add: "He helped us appreciate the rich meaning of life." And if I must choose one or a few of the types of meaning described in this book, they would be: knowledge, contribution, and family love.

Okay, now it's your turn.

APPENDIX

*None of the philosophies
except the religious ones
are able to satisfy men's
needs.*

*Abdulgani Abdulla
Deputy Chairman for
Soviet Islam*

SECULAR AND RELIGIOUS MEANING

I said in the first chapter that we would follow a road that has two dimensions—secular and religious. Looking one way, you see the secular dimension; looking another way, the religious. The table on the last page clarifies these two perspectives. Notice how the religious interpretation *adds* a relationship with a divine being.

Let me stress that this book is for both believers and non-believers. It includes both religion and philosophy insofar as both are about the meaning of life. The distinction between them is that religious faith begins with an assumption that science and philosophy can neither prove nor disprove; namely, that there is a divine, spiritual power who can somehow be communicated with. I don't ask you to believe in God, only to see the two perspectives.

A Divine Partner

For myself, I am a believer. I find something especially attractive about the religious option. The attraction consists in trusting that the meaning of life rests on a truly solid foundation—on something powerful, enduring, under-standing and communicative. This divine connection more than validates the essential attributes of meaning, namely: larger than self, personal, intelligible and purposeful.

I know my life would have meaning even if there were no God. I experience too much inner drive not to make my own meaning. I would probably survive solitary confinement. When my captors opened the cell door they would find me dancing or writing a poem in the dust. But I find meaning easier and richer when I believe in a divine person. That's because God does so much of the work. God makes a good partner in meaning—leading me on, challenging me, and holding it together when I'm not thinking about it. If they opened the cell door and found me crazed or dead, God would still be dancing.

Secular And Religious Meaning

	Secular Interpretation	Religious Interpretation
Love	To love family and special friends	... and God.
Being cared for	To know that someone special cares for me	... and this someone is God.
Treasure	To have and exchange beautiful, useful things	... which are gifts from a nurturing God.
Fair share	To have a fair share of this world's goods	... as bestowed by divine providence.
Sense of order	To live in a clean, orderly and rational way	... as a reflection of divine peace and order.
Achievement	To make or do something of value	... in imitation of the mighty and fruitful creator.
Contribution	To make the world a better place	... and so build God's Kingdom.
Adventure	To feel the excitement of action, journey and great events	... invited by God, and often with God as a participant.
Tradition	To relive what people have always done	... deeds which God has sanctioned and modeled.
Moral integrity	To do the right thing	... according to the law or counsel of God.
Salvation	To feel spared from some evil, weakness or addiction	... by the power and grace of God.
Presence	To be up and alive in the world	... grateful for being created by God.
Knowledge	To possess all being in one's mind	... sharing in God's wisdom.
Becoming	To incorporate many identities	... led by God to each.
Communion	To be one with Nature or all Being	... and with God.
Transcendence	To empty oneself, let-go, and accept what comes	... trusting all into the hands of God.

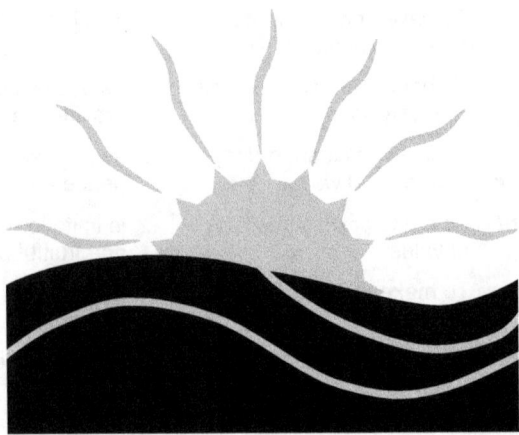

The End

POST SCRIPT

TOM KRAMLINGER   (1937 -2009)

Between the second and third printings of this book, Tom Kramlinger was diagnosed with pancreatic cancer. He lived for seven more months, fully engaged with work, family and friends. Knowing he could not get well, Tom sought meaning in his new situation. Reflecting on his life, Tom claimed his loves, blessings, values and accomplishments and concluded he'd surely had "more than his fair share." With gratitude and hope, Tom embraced transcendence. Letting go of all he loved, he entrusted himself to God and looked forward to whatever adventures might lie ahead.

Buried in Roselawn Cemetery, where his book begins, Tom is remembered with great love. A black marble stone proclaims:

Thomas L Kramlinger

Practical Philosopher

1937 + 2009